# THE MENToR

# THE

# MENTOR

## 15 Keys to Success in Sales, Business, and Life

# JACK CAREW

DONALD I. FINE BOOKS
*New York*

DONALD I. FINE BOOKS
Published by the Penguin Group
Penguin Putnam Inc., 375 Hudson Street,
New York, New York 10014, U.S.A.
Penguin Books Ltd, 27 Wrights Lane, London W8 5TZ, England
Penguin Books Australia Ltd, Ringwood, Victoria, Australia
Penguin Books Canada Ltd, 10 Alcorn Avenue,
Toronto, Ontario, Canada M4V 3B2
Penguin Books (N.Z.) Ltd, 182–190 Wairau Road,
Auckland 10, New Zealand

Penguin Books Ltd, Registered Offices:
Harmondsworth, Middlesex, England

First published by Donald I. Fine Books, an imprint of
Penguin Putnam Inc.

First Printing, January, 1998
10   9   8   7   6   5   4   3

 REGISTERED TRADEMARK—MARCA REGISTRADA

CIP data is available on request.
ISBN: 1-55611-541-5

Printed in the United States of America
Set in Goudy

This book is printed on acid-free paper. ∞

## Dedication

To the family—yours and mine—for their support, love, and devotion. Though the shape of the family has been transformed and molded by our ever-changing society, it remains the epicenter of all that is good, providing an anchor for us in our journey through life.

## Acknowledgments

This book is the result of a coming together of many people, many ideas, and many years of experience. Above all, I would like to thank all those wonderful people whose thoughts, words, and deeds have inspired this work. In particular, my devoted colleagues at Carew International and our loyal clients who have provided a solid foundation of support and validation.

I am especially indebted to my own mentor, Tom Costello, president and chief operating officer of ResourceNet International, whose wisdom, compassion and understanding of the human spirit have touched me in many positive ways. Though we have been friends and colleagues for more than thirty years, he never ceases to challenge my thinking, broaden my understanding, and deepen my appreciation of the human values that he has integrated into his life and his business.

And my special thanks to:

My son Kieran, whose subtle wizardry and vivid imagination helped shape this story. Kieran's spirit lives throughout *The Mentor*.

My wife, Barbara, for her loyalty and devotion; my son Sean and my daughter, Patty, for their love and support; my grandchildren for the joy and happiness they bring me.

Brenda Jones of Carew International, for her unselfish dedication to the project from beginning to end.

An exceptional publishing team—the late Donald I. Fine, senior vice president of sales and marketing Dick Heffernan of Penguin Putnam, and editor Tom Burke—all of whom championed this book from the very beginning.

Jeff Stewart and Diane Glynn, who nurtured the progress of this book and helped guide it into your hands with consummate skill and dedication.

Reverend George W. Rutler and Tom Monaghan, founders of Legatus, which has been a source of spiritual enrichment and renewal.

The gracious women of Mercy Center at Madison, Connecticut, for their encouragement and prayers during the writing of *The Mentor*.

Kurt Grossman, who is a dear friend to the Carew family.

Ed Claflin, an exceptional editor and writer, who is a model of positive values and integrity. Ed's valuable skills helped to make *The Mentor* a leadership model for everyone.

# CONTENTS

# A Word
# from the Author

In the last decade of the twentieth century, we have witnessed monumental commercial upheaval.

More has happened this decade—culturally, philosophically, and psychologically—to change the complexion of the workplace than happened in the three prior decades.

In the nineties, every organization has been bombarded with a host of bold new strategic initiatives. These include downsizing, reengineering, and restructuring—just to mention a few.

In some quarters these initiatives have robbed people of their future and some organizations of their souls. Hatchet men and women have come in and chopped up enterprises into new and more streamlined business models. And in the process, some of the older parts of the original model have been discarded, tossed on the junk heap.

Our heroes—and their wisdom—are gone.

Some of us have no mentors, and we have been called

upon to figure it all out for ourselves. Many of the young people entering business today have little in common with their leaders, and they suffer from their managers' inability to provide them with the wisdom and inspiration they crave.

Today's eager and promising professionals are thrown into the business arena without the human interaction skills they will need to overcome an uncertain future. While fluent in the technological fundamentals of their business, many lack confidence and competency when it comes to optimizimg the potential in their relationships with customers.

They have the words, but they haven't got the music. They can talk a good technical game, but they can't pull it off when it comes to influencing people, taking action, and creating change. They lack the magical ability to connect with other people whom they must influence.

This book is for the many gifted, courageous professionals who have been cast adrift and left to their own devices.

This book is about the human spirit and the possibilities in your relationships with others.

It is about unlocking the tremendous potential that exists in all of us.

—Jack Carew

# ✦✦✦ 15 Keys to Success ✦✦✦

## 1. LIFE IS A SALES CALL
*Everyone is selling somebody something. To be successful in selling, your beliefs have to become your cause.*

## 2. MAGNIFY YOUR SPIRIT
*The size of your commitment to the relationship multiplies and magnifies the potential for prosperity.*

## 3. EMBRACE THE TRUTH
*Each of us has a duty to be the business world's most vigorous advocate of truth. There is no health in us—and no future in our relationships—if we deceive our customers.*

## 4. ADMIRE YOURSELF FIRST
*To find the good in others, find the good in yourself.*

## 5. POWER UP WITH EXCITEMENT
*Passion is the magic that makes impossible-to-meet goals possible.*

## 6. COMPETE WITH ENERGY

*Competitiveness comes from the soul. It's a compelling desire to succeed. It's your ability to look down the barrel of a competitor's gun and not be intimidated but, rather, be motivated.*

## 7. ACHIEVE PREFERRED POSITION

*The core objective of all selling activity is to reach the position of maximum effectiveness and profitability with your customers. It's called Preferred Position.*

## 8. INFLUENCE THE OUTCOME

*If your spirit is missing from the meeting, your sales call will deteriorate into a conversation of good intent.*

## 9. DISCOVER THEIR DREAMS

*Asking high-return questions and listening to the customer's response is an advanced form of communication. It's the most important step in responding to the customer's call for help.*

## 10. RESOLVE WITH PASSION

*Make sure the customer feels your heart when you make your sales presentation. The customer will pay for your passion, because it is, after all, the best thing you have to sell.*

## 11. CLOSE WITH COURAGE

*Closing is a strategic moment that represents a test of courage and inner strength. Failing to close is not completing your mission.*

## 12. PERSIST WITH DETERMINATION

*It's not the competitor who decides whether you have won or lost. The only time you fail to make the sale is when you decide to stop the process.*

## 13. NEGOTIATE FROM STRENGTH

*In negotiations there can be no losers. The outcome has to be a win for all concerned. And fairness is the glue that keeps the process together—which means shared risk, shared commitment, and shared prosperity.*

## 14. BOUNCE BACK FROM REJECTION

*The business environment is an emotionally charged arena with exhilarating highs and crushing lows. Like injured athletes and exhausted performers, salespeople have to play when they're hurting.*

## 15. RENEW YOUR SOUL

*The forgiving human spirit is often brought to life in an angry customer—if you're quick to make amends.*

# MEETING THE MENTOR

Friday, six o'clock, and the rain falls in thin, even sheets outside the office window. Tim hangs up the phone, checks his voice mail and e-mail, and logs off for the night. With a sigh, he tucks a few disks inside his portable PC case, zips it up.

Specters of the past week float by. The sales call that *almost* produced new business. The frustration of trying to reach customers who wouldn't call back. A discouraging rejection—the loss of an old customer. A missed opportunity—where a competitor got a foot in the door.

Now the office is quiet—the week done. Everyone gone home. The phone no longer ringing.

It's confusing. Everything's a challenge—from planning new business to dealing with old problems that his predecessor left on the table. Is this what *every* person goes through on a new job? Or—and this is the thought that bothers him most, gnawing at his confidence—is he just not cut out to be a success in this profession?

Some say successful people are born, not made. If he's not a "born" salesperson, Tim wonders, will he ever hold the keys to success in his chosen profession?

"Tim?"

He looks up. Jill is standing in the door, her raincoat draped over one arm.

She smiles meekly. "You, too?"

"Me, too." He nods. "Look at this. . . ." He gestures toward the pile of message slips and proposals on the corner of his desk. "And not a single sale in the past two weeks."

"Yeah. Tell me about it." Jill's laugh sounds hollow.

The two of them started within a month of each other, and that in itself created a sort of boot camp bond between them. Like Tim, Jill had often had to rely on her own resources in the learning process—experiencing the exultation that came with new customer contacts, often followed by the disappointment of rejection. Each felt, in the other's presence, a kind of kinship and reassurance that arose from shared experiences and shared frustrations.

"I'm out of here. Enough is enough." Tim picks up his umbrella and briefcase, slings the strap of his PC case over his shoulder, and flicks off the light.

✦ ✦ ✦

Down the hall, the light from an open door falls across the industrial carpet. Tim shares a meaningful glance with Jill.

"Doesn't he *ever* go home?"

Jill shook her head. "I guess not. Mr. Stamina."

"I don't think it's stamina. There's something else that drives him."

Jill nods. From the expression on her face, Tim knows she is recalling her encounters with the man in the lighted office. Her contacts, like Tim's, have been brief but meaningful. The older man has the most distinguished business career of anyone they have ever known. Many in the company refer to him, with an affectionate kind of reverence, as the Wizard.

Tim and Jill, however, have given him another title. Brief as their encounters with the man have been, both experienced an immediate rapport—recognizing a warmth and sympathy, along with a kind of street-smart wisdom, that engendered immediate respect. They call him the Mentor.

✦　✦　✦

"Come on in."

Until that moment, Tim hardly realized that he and Jill had been drawn to the Mentor's door. They had only meant to say good night in passing—knowing that he must be very busy to be working so late, respectful of the time that the Mentor found for himself at the end of the day.

But the Mentor's smile was so immediate, his gesture so welcoming, that both Jill and Tim felt compelled to step inside and take the chairs that were offered.

Why had they come? These two young people hardly knew. Something had been lacking in their brief careers—that was for sure. Both of them certainly felt the need for guidance. Their manager had too many direct reports. He never seemed to have time for them.

Certainly, up to now, there had not been anyone around to counsel them day by day—to help them learn the ropes. Like so many of their young friends, they were in an environment that said as clearly as words, "You're on your own! It's every person for himself around here!"

Yet both realized they needed clearer guidance. In fact, the Mentor by his very presence offered something that might help provide what was lacking.

"Well—how's it going?" From anyone else, it would have been an inconsequential, almost dismissive question. But the Mentor's steady gaze and concentration told them, unmistakably, that there was no limit to his time and attentiveness.

To his own surprise, Tim found himself telling the older man everything about his past months of doubt, discouragement, and frustration. Of the strategies he'd tried. Of the calls he'd made—filled with energy and enthusiasm—only to find himself denied or rejected or, worst of all, not even seen.

From the way Jill nodded in agreement, Tim sensed that they were in accord. Whatever hesitancy she may have had in sharing her own feelings was overcome by Tim's forthrightness. Soon she was talking about the doubts she'd harbored about herself and her personal abilities—more doubts than she'd ever had before, about anything in her life.

She had felt totally prepared, totally ready when she started this job—and now, it was as if she were back in kindergarten. Why had no one told her it would be so difficult? Were she and Tim the only people in the world who had this kind of experience? And all these self-doubts—the way she took rejection so much to heart—was it really a sign that she didn't have what it took to become a high-achieving business professional?

And the Mentor listened. He listened with a kind of uncanny power to perceive, to acknowledge, to understand. At almost any point, Tim realized, the Mentor might have interjected his own views, his own experience, his own wisdom.

But he did not interrupt. He simply listened intently, now and then asking for clarification or nodding in acknowledgment, saying a word or two that prompted Tim and Jill to reveal still more—to tell the Mentor things they had admitted to no one, scarcely even to themselves.

When, finally, they were done, the Mentor regarded them in profound silence—a bemused expression on his face that made Tim feel as if his distress and discouragement were somehow understandable, acceptable, almost expected. For just an instant, Tim wondered whether he and Jill had said too much—whether they now looked foolish, unreliable, and incompetent in the Mentor's eyes.

But with the Mentor's next words, Tim's doubts vanished.

"You know there is nothing I can do for you," said the Mentor. "You can only do it for yourself. You have all the resources. You have begun to grasp the skills. I can assure you that if you continue to try, you will succeed."

He looked intently from Tim to Jill, then back again. "Fortunately, it's a path that many have gone down before."

"No one told me it would be so difficult!" The words burst from Tim like a cry for understanding. "It's so hard!"

"Yes," said the Mentor. "More difficult than anyone admits. But there's something you must remember. When you acquire a knowledge of selling, you are preparing yourself for the future."

The Mentor paused for a moment before continuing. "Selling will become the key to success, wealth, and prosperity in the twenty-first century. The skills of selling are no longer the exclusive domain of the sales professional. In this environment, *everyone* needs selling skills. Without those skills, careers will flounder, ideas will get lost, and projects will never come to fruition. Wherever you go, whatever you do, the selling skills you master will be your most valuable asset.

"In the years ahead," the Mentor continued, "we will continue to make the shift from a *few* people selling to *everyone* selling. That means everyone will have to assume the mantle of leadership and take the responsibility for securing loyal and profitable customers. And to do that, you must know The Way."

"Can you show us?" When he heard the eagerness in Jill's voice, Tim realized how intensely he felt it himself. How desperately he needed guidance, experience, understanding— why had he only realized it at this moment?

"If you are willing to bring everything to the task."

"What do you mean—*everything?*" Tim couldn't help feeling a jolt of fear. Up to now, this had all been a *job* to him— not a commitment or a vocation. And now, obviously, the Mentor was asking for something much more.

"I mean your heart as well as your head," said the Mentor. "We will talk of morality and ethics, of loyalty and truth, of commitment and friendship, of self-image and self-admiration. There will be spiritual matters and emotional matters. If you think these things are separable, if you think you can escape them, then this should not be your profession. But if you embrace these matters, if you can look deeply inside yourself and others and not be afraid, then perhaps I can guide you."

The Mentor seemed to pause for an eternity after these words—all the while keeping Tim and Jill under the steady, intense welcome of his gaze. But finally he asked the question that Tim had been wishing for—and half dreading.

"Do you want me to show you The Way?"

Tim found himself answering without hesitation, as if a force stronger than himself compelled him toward this commitment—a single word, "Yes!" And as if it were the echo of his own voice, Jill's reply was the same, so instinctive and spontaneous that it brought a smile to the Mentor's lips.

"Then let us begin."

# CHAPTER 1

# LIFE IS A SALES CALL

# The Key to Selling

*Everyone is selling somebody something. To be successful in selling, your beliefs have to become your cause.*

"No one told me what to expect when I found myself selling," said Tim. "One minute I feel like I'm starting to learn what's what—and the next instant, something happens to remind me that I'm just a beginner. No one except those in selling seems to realize how challenging it is."

"I suspect that many people simply don't understand the nature of selling—much less understand the challenges we face," said the Mentor. "Selling is the defining function within any commercial enterprise. The sales effort makes all other activity possible. It's the gateway to prosperity. Yet the historical view of sales involves many negative stereotypes.

"But things are changing," continued the Mentor. "I think everyone is waking up to the fact that they have to sell. Now the sales process is being legitimized by 'nontraditional' pockets of sales activity. Selling occupies central position on the world's economic stage.

"Consider this: A coach sells his athletes on being 'game

ready.' A politician sells his platform to the electorate. Every physician has to sell his 'get-well therapy prescription' to the patient. Mothers and fathers sell their kids on the importance of education, and teachers are selling students on the benefits of study and hard work. And everywhere you turn, you'll find employers selling employees on the benefits of producing quality products.

"It seems that no matter what you do in life, you've got a customer you have to sell. And what are you selling? You're selling your point of view, or a recommended course of action, or a proposition. People are selling causes and solutions, or the need to take action. Sometimes what you're selling is your *passion* about your ideas, beliefs, or recommendations.

"And the people to whom you're selling wear many hats. Some are clients, consumers, or any kind of prospective buyers. But there are many other customers. Users of our products or services, patients, investment panels, procurement officers, management committees, task teams, special interest groups—these are all customers.

"As we find ourselves at the beginning of the twenty-first century, we're seeing newfound respect for the role of sales in every professional sphere. Architects, chemists, attorneys, engineers, management consultants—all are discovering that they have to sell. In our world the extent and rapidity of change is astounding—but great organizations will always need people who can sell. Selling therefore is an honored place. And to be successful in the twenty-first century, you will have to have the mind of a computer and the soul of a saint."

The Mentor paused for a moment, considering his next

words carefully. "You know, selling provides the fuel for a company's future."

"I guess I'm in the right place, then," said Tim eagerly. "I find making a new business development call on a new customer as exciting as Neil Armstrong's first step on the moon. It's *incomparably* exciting. For me it's a mystical moment."

The Mentor regarded Tim with a smile. "If you really feel that thrill, then I'd say you've got the right attitude. And taking your customer's best interest into consideration is central to your success. To the customer, you could be the shining beacon of hope. If you have a distaste for selling, it can cripple your efforts to influence change. It can make you older before your time. For all of us who treat our profession as a passion, life is one great big sales call. The excitement never wears off."

"And when you finally get the customer's business—!" Jill exclaimed.

The Mentor nodded in agreement. "To someone who loves selling, there's nothing that can't be cured with, 'Yes, I vote for you.' It's like hitting the lottery."

"Sure, but that's only the good half," Tim said skeptically.

Jill nodded in agreement as she added, "Some sales are so dangerous, I feel like I have to wear body armor."

"No one operates with impunity when they're selling," the Mentor agreed. "There are good or bad consequences for every move you make. It's your personal actions that decide the outcome of events.

"In selling, you don't get points for artistic impression," the Mentor continued. "There's no such thing as a moral victory or a Spirit of the Game Award. When was the last time a customer turned you down but said, 'We appreciate your hard work. Stay in touch. Keep calling on us'? In sports, you get points for coming in second. In politics, you have some assurance that you will hold on to your seat or finish your term in office. In selling, there are no such guarantees."

"I used to think it was all instinct," Jill reflected. "But it's not. It's a great game of concentration, emotion, and momentum."

"That's right," the Mentor agreed. "Many people don't realize that selling is science and art—and you need to learn both. I remember how I started out, thinking it was easy. I used to be a young man in a big hurry—but it wasn't long before I was in over my head and choking on my dust. In fact—" He paused, shaking his head at a grim, distant memory. "I'll never forget the endearing words my first boss said to me."

"What were they?" asked Jill.

"He said I approached my sales activities like a salaried tourist—and he assured me that my next raise would not become effective until *I* did. He said I mistook activity for accomplishment. He told me that I created a flurry of work, but with very little payoff in terms of results."

"And I thought *my* boss was tough," Tim remarked with a laugh.

"You have no chance to practice *before* you start selling," the Mentor observed. "When you find yourself facing a new business development opportunity, you're playing with live ammunition from the very beginning."

"And it's terrible to admit that you don't know what to do," Jill put in. "Especially when your stomach tells you that things aren't going well."

The Mentor nodded. "When I'd had my fill of failed attempts, I would seek the safe havens of the computer screen or office—or the comforting security of spending time with old, established customers.

"For selling, you need to call up all your inner reserves," the Mentor continued. "You know, many people who underrate selling simply don't recognize the incredible complexity and challenge of this vital activity."

He thought a moment before adding, "Selling is a journey. Even if you win a dozen times, you cannot think that you have 'arrived'—that you have mastered the art and science. It's more than networking and schmoozing. You won't win with gimmicks and catchy slogans. It's a socio-emotional enterprise that requires the use of all of your psychological capital."

The Mentor paused to consider his next words. "Success in selling requires bold vision, imagination, and the courage to create your own miracles.

"Selling is the art of the possible—what can be versus what *can't* be," the Mentor went on. "If you are successful at selling, people will expect great things from you. They'll expect you to be the person who can handle anything. Successful people normally can."

"Some people just don't have that kind of success orientation," said Tim. "It's not in their nature."

"Maybe not," responded the Mentor. "But I can tell you there's a great difference between *thinking about* success and *working* for it."

"What do you mean?"

"Often, businesspeople who are told they have to sell as part of their job simply *think* about success. But the dead-serious ones *find ways to succeed*. Today, it's the ones who are finding ways to succeed that are setting themselves apart from the rest. They are like ambassadors."

"But some people dislike the competitive nature of selling," said Tim. "They think they're above it. And some are frightened to death by the prospect of having to sell something."

The Mentor shrugged. "Like it or not, selling is a game of winners and losers—people who expect to excel, and those who act as if they were destined to fail. Much of selling is an adversarial contest where you have to beat out someone else to win the prize. There's very seldom a second place. It means that you take something away from someone else—specifically, your rival.

"Selling is a high-stakes contest that takes a lot of desire and endurance. You have to come to the competitive arena ready to play. And you have to keep ahead of your competitors.

"Like any other competitive activity, selling has an emotional price tag attached to it. You have to be emotionally fit to make that purchase.

"It's inevitable that you will suffer defeats and become discouraged—but better that than to go through life without ever knowing victory or defeat. So in selling, you can expect to have your share of ups and downs. That's when you need unbridled hope and a strong competitive nature to succeed."

"I've taken it on the chin a few times already," Tim confirmed. "If someone could paint what's in my head after a discouraging discussion with a customer, it would be a pretty bleak picture."

Jill laughed. "I keep saying to myself, 'Get tough, Jill, get tough. Grow another layer of skin!' I guess I'm hoping I'll get thick-skinned before I get wounded."

"We all go through that," the Mentor acknowledged. "From time to time, you'll be faced with some unpleasant choices and consequences. If you are out there selling long enough, you will see everything—and you will get scarred. The harsh reality of selling is that you will face fear, uncertainty, and disappointment on a frequent basis. You have to live with anxiety bearing down on you all the time.

"You are never immune to the anxieties and frustrations that accompany dealing with people. It's the critical component of the job. No matter how important or distant and removed the decision-makers are, they are still human beings and subject to emotions—love, hate, joy, fear, and disappointment—just like you. To be successful at selling, you have to work with these emotions that have historically resulted in separation.

"Selling can be tough for the weak of heart. Sooner or later, you are sure to take your lumps. So on some days you will need all of your resources to help you get through some tough times."

"But there's another side of the coin," Tim interjected. "What about the thrill you get when new opportunities come up—and you *know* you can meet the challenge!"

"And the opportunities are always available if you have the desire and ambition to look for them," the Mentor agreed. "In fact, if you're given sales responsibilities, you're actually being commissioned an Opportunity Manager. To earn that title, you have to show skill combined with courage in the discharge of your responsibilities. It's more than people-pleasing: It's shoulder-to-shoulder hard work toward a prized common goal.

"In this new era, when everyone needs to sell, all of us have customers, and we are all in the customer business—not the order-taking business. You personally are as much a part of the deal as the ideas and solutions you sell.

"Victory in selling is measured in the number of customers who continue to pay a premium price for your recommendations because they value *you* as a premium," the Mentor went on. "Having you on their team is more valuable than having your rival, who is selling his solutions at a lower price."

The Mentor paused and leaned back in his chair, lost in a moment's reflection. Looking from Tim to Jill, he continued, "The quality of the messenger is as important as the quality of the message. Your knowledge is your capital: Your knowledge of the customer's human as well as business needs and your passion in presenting your solution are your lifeline to success."

"You know, I think I need to do some attitude adjustment," observed Tim.

"What do you mean?" asked the Mentor.

"Up to now, I've been thinking of sales as an entry level position—getting my foot in the door, so to speak. But selling is more than a way up the ladder. It *is* the ladder."

The Mentor laughed in agreement. "You're right, it is. Unfortunately, many people don't know how many rungs there are in that ladder—or even how to take the next step."

"Can you tell us?" asked Jill.

"Well, everyone's experience is different," the Mentor replied.

"But we have to begin somewhere," Jill insisted.

"Yes, you do." The Mentor reflected a moment. "It's not easy to put all these ideas into words. But I'll try."

The Mentor paused a moment longer. Then he outlined the first steps of The Way.

## ✦✦✦ THE WAY ✦✦✦

✔ **Use your uniqueness.**

What you do and how you do it is distinct and special. People are buying the conviction and passion for your cause that they see burning in your eyes. Let your example tell the whole story. Get them to want you first and what you are selling next. Be the benefit.

✔ **Be turned on by the excitement of converting others to your beliefs.**

Do this by becoming a vital component in your customer's vision for the future. Your very presence should create wealth and prosperity for the customer's enterprise. Your customer's success will be your success.

✔ **Mobilize your resources.**

If you are going to reach glory land in selling, it will be on the backs of the support people who execute the details of your agreement. They are the ones who carry the business over the finish line. Take care of them, and they will surely take care of you and—most important—your customer.

✔ **Be a luminary.**

In the future, you will have to appeal to more people more rapidly in an ever-changing world if you want to compete in the contest to win. Never relax. Be ambitious. Every day of your working life, rededicate yourself to learning more and getting better. Become a luminary that people can come to for guidance and inspiration. It will give you a decided competitive advantage.

✔ **Decide for yourself.**

All of us have a capacity for greatness, but having it and using it are two different things. In the final analysis, you decide how successful you are going to be at selling. And in selling, you are at your very best when you are doing something good for someone else—your customer.

✦ ✦ ✦

"Everything you've said about selling seems true," Tim observed when the Mentor was finished. "But still, there are times when I feel like I'm engaged in an artificial, people-pleasing activity."

"Not at all," responded the Mentor. "In selling, you will discover endless challenges, complexities, and rewards in *rela-*

*tionships*. But if that's going to happen, you need *anam cara* with your customers."

"*Anam cara?* What's that?" asked Jill.

The Mentor smiled. "Maybe I'm getting ahead of myself. Let me explain."

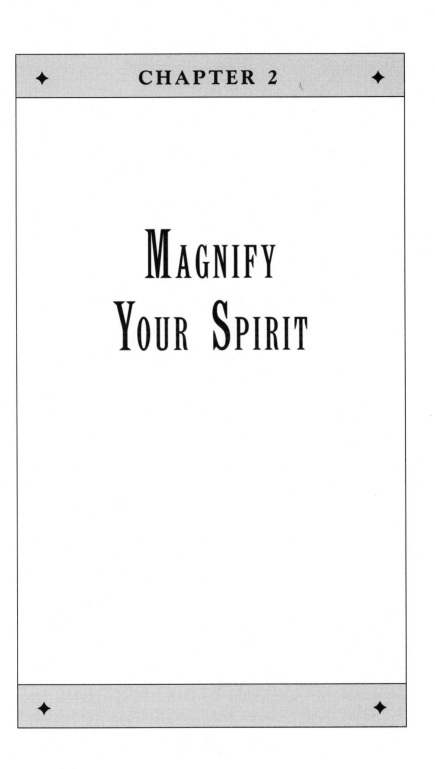

CHAPTER 2

# MAGNIFY YOUR SPIRIT

# The Key to Successful Relationships

*The size of your commitment to the relationship multiplies and magnifies the potential for prosperity.*

"At first, like you, I wondered whether I was just in the business of pleasing people," the Mentor recalled. "I asked myself whether I had to be Johnny-on-the-Spot for the customer at all times. I met experienced business professionals in midcareer who still maintained that frame of mind.

"Some so-called relationships are nothing more than commercial obligations. The customer is in great need of what you sell and ultimately buys from you out of severe necessity. This kind of relationship isn't long for this world. It's headed toward a state of considerable apathy and will eventually evaporate.

"For selling to become a lifelong love, you must be able to find joy in building *helping* relationships with others. It is from this joy that you will discover the goodness in each other and a wellspring of gratification, validation, and productivity."

The Mentor paused a moment, reflecting. "In Celtic spiritual tradition, there's a concept of the human spirit that spoke to me very profoundly about the nature of friendship. That concept is *anam cara*.

"The Celts believed that a soul shines all around the body," the Mentor went on. "They described it as 'a luminous cloud.' I call it a special kind of unity. And when you are very open and trusting with another person, your two souls are connected. This is what they call *anam cara*—a friendship so strong that when you are blessed with it, the bond of two committed people magnifies and multiplies the potential for growth and prosperity. My friend John O'Donohue, an Irish poet and priest who has studied the spiritual roots of Celtic worship, described it this way: 'Your *anam cara* always beholds your light and beauty, and accepts you for who you truly are.' "

The Mentor leaned forward, and his voice took on an added note of seriousness. "Selling takes generosity and a total commitment to the welfare of the customer. If I have *anam cara* with you, I am available to you at many levels. I will always operate in your total best interest and only influence you to do the right thing. I care about your *total* well-being.

"When you experience joy, I experience joy, and when you suffer, I suffer. If I have *anam cara* with you, I'm going to see the good in you and be patient with you when you need me to be. I'll make your friends my friends because they're important to you.

"*Anam cara* represents my deepest commitment. It means I will transcend my ego, and I will make a gift of myself to you. It means I want to know as much about you as I can because I delight in your spirit. I will lend you a receptive ear and an open heart."

The Mentor paused to consider his own words.

"I firmly believe that you must take the leadership role in optimizing the potential for *anam cara*. It's your responsibility to take the first steps in creating *anam cara*. This is where the confluence of your and your customer's interests results in connectedness, synergy, and productivity. *Anam cara* is the foundation for all other keys to successful selling. It touches the core belief that identifies us as true professionals."

Tim felt confusion assault him like a wave. Wasn't the business of selling, after all, a matter of transacting goods or services in exchange for payment? So far, the Mentor had said nothing of this.

On the contrary, the Mentor spoke as if the relationship was *everything*. And how could Tim take responsibility for so many relationships? Wouldn't it be overwhelming—exhausting—impossible? Did he even want to bother?

"What must I do?" he inquired with a feeling of helplessness.

"If you want to be truly connected to your customers, the key is *caring*," said the Mentor. "When you truly care, your customer's 'inner knower' will sense this phenomenon. You will have created an environment where the customer is in the spotlight. And when you're paying attention to the customer, you're paying attention to the business.

"Winning people over to your side is done simply by trying to see things from their side. It's called 'listening to understand.' This will enable you to actively participate in the life of the customer. You will be successful at working with customers if you manage to keep your attention focused on their fears, their needs, their hopes, their aspirations.

"Regrettably, inwardly focused people want to be center stage all the time. They're emotionally disconnected from the customer, and as a result, their ideas do not register with the customer."

"But the relationship *can't* be everything," said Tim. "There's information I have to get to the customer—technical details, application procedures, costs—"

"Of course." The Mentor sounded almost impatient. "I am assuming you have a firm grip on the functional aspects of your recommended solution, and you will give the customer the benefit of that knowledge. But you have to be hypersensitive to the human side of the relationship as well as the technical side.

"I remember the words of a rabbi who told me, 'If you get completely wrapped up in your own psychic energy, you may miss the excitement of others.' If you are not open and accepting, you do not give others the gift of creating a bond with you. When you are selfish, you are not guided by the truth. All of your actions will be geared to serve your purpose and not the other person's.

"Some businesspeople are so analytical and technically focused that they have a severe aversion to high-expression, relationship-building activities. If you play your technical card to the exclusion of taking a personal interest in your customer, you demonstrate indifference. Even if you don't create a rapid breakdown in the relationship, you'll be putting it at risk.

"Customers often ask the questions, 'Will you be there in the morning? Will you be around when I need you? Will you rescue me when the wheels come off? Will you restore order when things go awry?' These are legitimate concerns. Don't cast doubt on your sincerity by not paying as much attention to the relationship *after* you acquire the customer's business. Maintain a constant and vigilant presence with the customer that goes beyond the duration of the business agreement. *Be there* for your customers and they will surely be there for you over the long haul. This gives you an excellent opportunity to build an enduring, true friendship and enables you to expand and broaden your influence and create a loyal following."

"You've described everything I want to do," said Tim. "But how?"

The Mentor smiled at his eagerness. "I would say you're ready for the next steps of The Way."

"Yes," Tim replied with a nod.

The Mentor thought a moment in silence. Then he began.

## ✦✦✦ THE WAY ✦✦✦

✔ **Look for the best in others.**

There is no such thing as a bad customer. All customers are good—some are just "gooder" than others. With some you have *anam cara*, and with others you're still working on it. In any case, remember that customers occasionally make the wrong choices, and sometimes, perhaps, their treatment of you is simply that—a wrong choice.

No matter how disgruntled you feel, never speak

poorly of a customer in the presence of others. It is courting bad luck. Instead, rediscover the goodness in that customer and let the other person's goodness be your focus. These deep feelings will bring you closer to one another.

✔ **Let go of the "me first" attitude.**

Strive to deepen every friendship. To wish for the good of another person is always good luck. And that's what you're doing when you want the best for your customers.

Actively participate in the customer's life by paying attention to what's important to that person at the human level. If you are totally wrapped up in your own self-interest, you could be guilty of egotism, self-worship, and selfishness. You will miss the excitement of others. As a matter of fact, you won't even know they're around. Talk to the customer about things that are important to him—his view of the world, his hope for the future, his dreams, his needs, his life.

✔ **Listen! It's the best way you can say you care.**

The act of listening says to the customer, "Right now, your concerns and feelings are more important to me than my own." Listening to understand helps you shake off the shackles of your own self-preoccupation. It's the same as saying, "I am interested, I care, and I want to help."

Listening to understand is the brick and mortar of *anam cara*.

✔ **Forgive and forget.**

Not all relationships are mistake-free. Sometimes a healing has to take place in a relationship if it is going to survive. Just as you can't forget if you won't forgive, you can't have a future working relationship if there is bitterness and resentment lingering from the past.

Make a crisis the source of your strength. Approach your customer with an olive branch. This deep commitment to the relationship will build *anam cara* and forge a bond that withstands tough times.

It will teach you tolerance and wisdom. It will prepare you for your next great challenge—and that may have nothing to do with selling.

✔ **Become the "coin of the realm."**

Position yourself to be the obvious choice for doing business. Create such an outstanding customer-focused presence that people carry you around in their souls. This effort will create a positive, permanent image and will strengthen your *anam cara*. This value-based relationship will provide you with a strong defense against your rivals.

✦ ✦ ✦

"I know some people who actually try to remove the human element when you interact with them," said Jill. "It seems like they need to depersonalize the relationship for fear that you will take advantage of their good-naturedness."

"That's true," said the Mentor. "There are some people who avoid deep relationships because they are not comfortable when they have to deal with each other at the human level. In some cases, such people have gone from personal-proximity to electronic-proximity relationships. You know what I mean: They prefer communicating with you via e-mail messages rather than looking you in the eye."

"Is there any way to bridge that gap?" asked Tim.

"You need to establish trust," the Mentor said emphatically. "Trust is the fabric of all relationships. It is the centerpiece of *anam cara*. With trust, all things are possible."

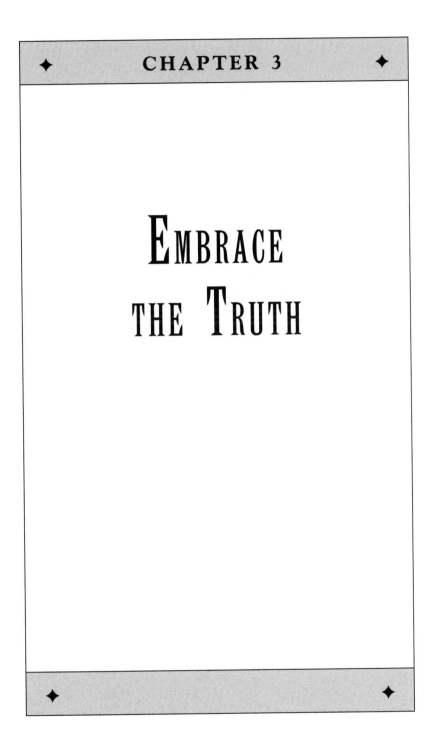

# CHAPTER 3

# EMBRACE THE TRUTH

# The Key to Establishing Trust

*Each of us has a duty to be the business world's most vigorous advocate of truth. There is no health in us—and no future in our relationships—if we deceive our customers.*

"You know, there are times when I come very close to saying things I don't really mean," Tim reflected. "My heart's in the right place—" He shook his head. "But there are times I make promises I'm not sure I can keep because I have to count on others."

Jill agreed vigorously. "It can all happen so fast—in the heat of the moment. I don't mean to deceive anyone with outright malarkey. I never want to lie to the customer. But sometimes I'm tempted to make promises. And I have to say to myself, 'No, Jill, don't do it. Don't make that promise until you know you can keep it.'"

"I'd advise you to listen to that inner voice," said the Mentor. "You might be tempted to raise expectations, but I guarantee you will pay the price if you fail to deliver on your word.

"The centerpiece in a businessperson's code of conduct is integrity—to always operate in the customer's best interest. If you're going to do that, you have an obligation to the truth. Truth cannot be sacrificed for the benefit of the business.

"We often find ourselves having to make pivotal choices that reflect our sense of honesty," the Mentor continued. "I believe that people who deceive and lie are guilty of malpractice. They've lost their way—and their actions could impeach the credibility of them *and* their organization. In selling, the truth is not optional—it's mandatory.

"Chronic liars are the dregs of commercial society. If you're not acting with integrity, it's more than a serious flaw in character or a broken pledge. It's more like a big, black hole."

The Mentor regarded Tim and Jill with serious eyes before he went on. "You have a personal responsibility to make sure your actions match your words. Make the truth your most important priority. It is your soul that oversees the debate going on inside you. Listen to your soul.

"It's the journey of life that shapes our souls. The values you develop as a young kid, when your character is still being formed, will be the basis around which you will act out your adult life. But your values can always change for the better. You can replace negative values with good values by hanging around value-rich people. Remember, your character is shaped by the choices you make.

"But if you are overcome by the need for material goods, recognition, and power, you are likely to bend the truth. An overabundance of selfishness, blind ambition, and fear of not getting what you want will sometimes cause you to make the fatal error of lying to the customer.

"And when you're caught in a deception, it could be your ticket out of the relationship. Deception sets up a wall of separation."

"I *never* set out to be dishonest," observed Jill. "It's just that I get very enthusiastic and—well, sometimes I get carried away. I start to believe we can do *anything* for the customer, and then I have to pull back and ask myself, 'Wait, Jill, what are you *promising*?'"

"And that's exactly what you *should* be asking," the Mentor agreed. "There are times when we reach a threshold moment—when we must choose between bending the truth or telling it like it is. Naturally you're excited about your unique response to the customer's needs. You've got that infectious enthusiasm, Jill—and you want to make the sale. All laudable impulses.

"The trouble is, the customer will have a crisis of confidence and you'll be viewed as seriously flawed if you don't keep your word. You can't airbrush out a deception. And a *pattern* of lying can derail your career before it gets started. It will rob you of your future."

"Sometimes I actually have to check my words," Jill observed. "Otherwise, I'll end up asking myself, 'Jill—what have you done?'"

"It's good you've discovered that now," said the Mentor. "Some people get into an unconscionable pattern of 'sell and repent.' They come dangerously close to manufacturing the truth, promising the customer something they can't possibly deliver. And they justify their actions by convincing themselves that somehow, someway, they *can* deliver. Even though in their gut they know it's a pipe dream.

"To not tell the truth is to create a climate of sadness. If you break a pledge, it leaves an emotional scar with the customer that will cost you dearly. The customer will not look at you with a kind eye."

"It sounds like an absolute," Tim observed.

"It is," the Mentor replied. "There is an immutable connection between truth and selling. You're the person who forges an alliance between the customer and the provider— and you're the person who secures and sustains the relationship. If you're caught in a deception, you have a moral crisis on your hands. It can ruin you."

The Mentor hesitated a moment, reflecting. Obviously, his own words had unveiled some unwanted memory.

"I remember an incident—long ago," the Mentor recalled, his expression still clouded. "I had a chance at some business that was absolutely brilliant. It was exactly what the company needed and wanted badly. And I needed it to hit my numbers for the year.

"The customer said, 'The business is yours if you can guarantee me that you can work with a short implementation deadline and guarantee me a problem-free start-up.'

"The need in me for this business was so intense that I gushed forth with a hopeful, 'I can do it! I can get it done!'

"Deep down inside, I knew I didn't have a tinker's chance in hell of pulling it off. But I took the chance with the intent of moving heaven and earth in order to meet my customer's demands. I rationalized that decision by convincing myself that somehow, someway, I would prevail."

The Mentor shook his head. "Prevail I did not, and, yes, I paid a severe penalty. But worse yet, so did the customer.

"I opted for the short-term gain, but instead wound up with a long-term loss—the customer's future business. The *anam cara* left the relationship, and my position with the customer took a turn for the worse. The customer was finished with me."

The Mentor contemplated Jill and Tim as he added, "I didn't know how important honesty was to me until I came close to losing it. Then I realized that deception erodes the moral dimension of your life.

"As I look back on that incident, I have to ask myself, 'What was going through my head?' It's hard to name everything—fear, anxiety, hopefulness, optimistic determination. But it all comes down to this: In the heat of the moment, I made the wrong call."

"But that happens," Jill insisted. "It's so hard to keep a cool head and make the right call all the time."

"I agree," said the Mentor. "When you're laden and over-burdened with passion and preoccupation, you may make the wrong choice because you haven't thought about it. But you'll be a broken person if you deceive the customer—and you're deceiving him if you give the customer inaccurate, incomplete, or unreliable information. Crossing the line is a major act of selfishness; it satisfies your needs at the expense of others.

"You will have to repair yourself and the relationship if you're going to have a future with the customer you let down. The passage of time defuses the impact of poor quality, lateness, poor execution, and mismanagement—but it may not wipe out the stinging impact of a deception."

"And it's almost worse to get away with it," Tim observed.

The Mentor nodded his agreement. "That's when you have to ask yourself, 'What's going on in my inner world?' When you're at this kind of crossroads, you face an internal struggle. Many elements are involved in that struggle—the company you keep, the values you embrace, and the lessons you learned in life that speak out to you. Strict adherence to the truth is a life choice."

"If lying becomes a pattern . . ." Jill began.

But the Mentor anticipated her. "If you are a repeat offender, you're digging your own grave. You'll be guilty of moral drift. Lying and deception destabilize a relationship. If you're bending the truth, you're walking a tightrope. One's suitability to be a salesperson is over if his deceptions are chronic.

"Manufacturing the truth to suit yourself is like committing commercial suicide. It is an offense against everything we stand for as sales professionals—the customer's best interests. When you deceive a customer, you are tainted. It will be difficult for people to trust you in the future—that is, if they can get over your deception.

"A lie is like stealing from your customer—stealing the confidence he placed in you. Lying is putting your own ambitions before the other person's. And when you're caught in a lie, the offended party will cry foul. Bitterness and disillusion will set in if you're caught in the deception.

"When the customer has been a victim of your deception," the Mentor continued, "his doubts will be looming in the background, and he will lay down severe conditions for reentry."

"I can't imagine trying to patch up the relationship if that happens. Your whole position could become unraveled," said Jill.

"There will be strict penalties," the Mentor agreed. "Even if you're not cashiered immediately, it will certainly hasten your departure and it might even cause irreversible damage to the relationship. Your *anam cara* is on the line.

"Deception is a desperate act of selfishness and doom that

could deal the relationship a mortal blow. And salespeople who deceive their customers can expect a long, hard fall from grace. The relationship will grow cold and distant. The customer's office turns into no-man's-land in a hostile environment. And your critics will be calling for your head—especially those who are most negatively affected by your actions. You could be in for savage reprisals."

The Mentor looked from Tim to Jill. "There is no right way to do the wrong thing. If you do the wrong thing, your career is in trouble because it's headed in the wrong direction.

"If a customer catches you in a deception but doesn't disown you, he might be just hanging on, that's all. You're forcing the customer into making an unacceptable choice—between you and the truth.

"Remember, people must have faith that you're telling the truth. You're the guardian and the steward of the relationship. Truth is an act of will. You'll shatter their confidence if you deceive them.

"The customer will become increasingly skeptical if he thinks you are not telling the whole story. Lying is validating the customer's worst fear—'I really can't depend upon this person to do his best for me.' It's a sobering reality that he'll always be looking over his shoulder, and he'll have zero tolerance for deception in the future."

"Isn't there any way to come back?" Tim wondered aloud.

"Nothing can be so bad that it's an unforgivable offense—even if it's an unforgettable offense," the Mentor answered. "Anybody who's out there working is going to make a mistake from time to time. Everyone is entitled to at least a second chance."

"And if she *does* get a second chance—then what?" asked Jill.

"You cannot move forward unless you have come to terms with what you have done in the past. At some point, you have to come to grips with the seriousness of your act.

"Reach into yourself and bring the good person that you are out into the light of day. This might influence the offended party to treat you with dignity, compassion, and forgiveness. There's a good chance you will emerge from the darkness of untruth and experience new and vigorous growth.

"Nevertheless, admitting the truth can be painful medicine. It's a delicate situation—a fragile state of affairs," the Mentor observed. "Once the magic is gone, you're working at a disadvantage. It's a crisis situation—and you have to be earnest in making things right.

"And yet, trust *can* be restored. Everyone is worthy of forgiveness unless they are a repeat offender. How you go about assuring your customer that a deception will never happen again is just as important as your contrition. You have to take certain steps in order to return to the good graces of your customer."

And then he told them how.

## ✦✦✦ THE WAY ✦✦✦

 **Acknowledge your need for forgiveness.**

The relationship between you and your customer will be at a crossroads. But ask yourself the core question, "What would the customer want me to do now that I've *reached* the crossroads?" Almost always, the customer will say, "Give it to me straight. Tell me the truth."

That could be the beginning of the way back to redemption, which overcomes the dark cloud hanging over your shoulder. You become renewed, redeemed, released, set free, made new, and made whole.

### ✔ Don't let the clock run out.

Offer an apology as quickly as you can. Don't wait until it's too late. The penitential season in your life—when you are making amends—should come quickly. Atone for your mishap. Give your word that the incident will not be repeated—and keep your word.

### ✔ Suffer yourself into healing.

The saving behavior is contrition and a firm resolution not to lie in the future. Feelings of guilt, shame, remorse, and fear are normal, natural, and necessary. They're part of the inner healing process. Don't deny these feelings, because there is a redemptive value in suffering. It helps you purge yourself of negative feelings, and it helps you begin atonement.

### ✔ Enlist a friend.

Talk to a good friend. Telling someone about the mishap will give you some relief. In all likelihood, they will remind you of the good and honest person you really are. Take that affirmation and let it propel you into a forward-focused action plan, coming clean with yourself and making amends. This will help you get refocused and begin the process of rebuilding the relationship.

✔ **Clean the slate.**

To make amends, admit the deception, acknowledge the criticism, express regret, and make a firm resolution that this behavior will not reoccur. If you misled the customer, you have to fess up and take your lumps. You'll need to work hard to reverse the image the customer has of you.

If you want to get back into the customer's good graces, you have to be patient. It's the American way to give a person a second chance. But it will take time. If the customer lets you back in, he will probably do so only after he is assured you will honor the confidence that he has placed in you. Then it's up to you.

✔ **Find ways to rebuild trust.**

Remember, trustworthiness is predictability. It means that the customer can depend upon you. If you continue to behave in ways that bring your integrity into question, no one will see you as reliable. You don't want your customer guessing what you're going to do next. Be consistent, predictable, and, above all, honest. Honesty is liberating. The wonderful truth keeps everything level.

✔ **Trust in the goodness of others.**

Disasters are reversible. Oftentimes, the customer takes you off the hook and gives you yet another chance. Be forthright and say, "I'm sad and sorry this happened to our relationship." Don't give up on the forgiving human spirit in others or in your own ability to get up and get on with it!

✔ **Embrace the truth.**

Adopt honesty and integrity as your core values. Believe me when I say that these values become more precious to you as you live another day. See it as your sacred obligation to stand against the collapse of values and morality in your profession. If you are faithful to the truth, you will become a person of great integrity and immense stature.

✦　✦　✦

"You know, when we restore trust and integrity, we're not just doing it for the sake of business," the Mentor mused. "We're doing it for ourselves."

"I've found that I can't kid myself," Jill agreed. "I have to be able to rely on my own judgment."

"Some call it self-respect," the Mentor said. He thought for a moment before adding, "I think I prefer to call it self-admiration. It's another element of *anam cara*," the Mentor explained, "and strange as it may seem, self-admiration may be the most important element of all."

Suddenly the Mentor's expression became more somber,

and when he spoke again, he sounded more reflective than ever before. "You know, it's only the previous inconsistencies in my own life that allow me to talk about truth and trust with the voice of experience. Pure selfishness, fear of losing, or an overactive need for instant gratification—for something I desperately wanted—caused me to act foolishly and inconsistently early on.

"But no one is immune from the temptations to make the wrong choice," the Mentor went on. "There's always the temptation to take the self-serving bait or swallow the self-indulgent hook and do what's most important to you at the moment."

As the Mentor lifted his eyes to Tim and Jill, they saw a bright smile light his features as he added, "There is no sanctuary for deception—but there is redemption. You are not necessarily mortally wounded. So when you are forgiven, *act* forgiven."

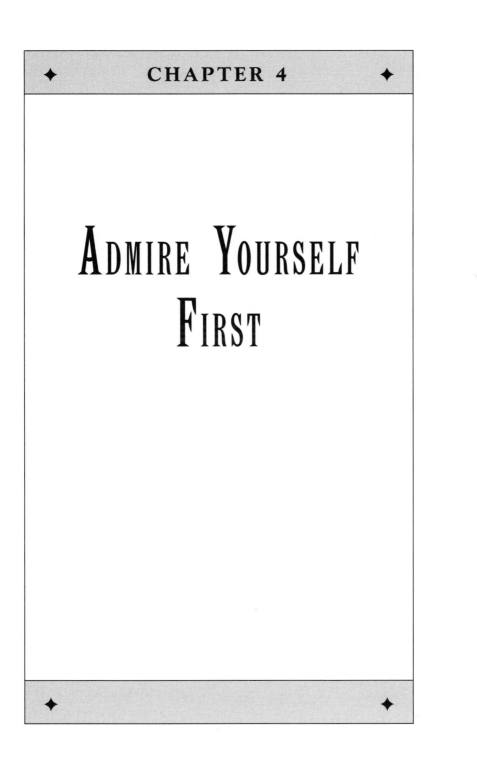

CHAPTER 4

# ADMIRE YOURSELF FIRST

# The Key to Achieving Self-Admiration

◆ *To find the good in others, find the good in yourself.* ◆

Turning to the Mentor, Jill asked a question that had been preying on her mind for months.

"I've heard that salespeople are *born*, not *made*. Do you think that's true?"

Tim broke in with a laugh. "I'll bet that's *my* problem. I just wasn't born for this job!"

The Mentor shook his head at Tim's words. Leaning forward, he studied both of the young salespeople for a moment before he replied, "It's my belief that salespeople are not born and they are not made, either. They *evolve*. They learn through trial and illuminating experiences. They learn when they receive guidance, take risks, and make discoveries. Once they get a couple of successes under their belts, they repeat those successes until they become successful habits. And a habit is a good act done often. For them, difficulty brings experience, and from experience comes wisdom."

---

"Well, I don't feel like I'm learning fast enough," said Tim. "Sometimes I'm dealing with PSD."

"PSD—what's that?" asked Jill.

"Permanent Self-Doubt." Tim managed a wan smile. "I keep asking myself, 'What am I doing wrong?' "

"Perhaps you're not doing *anything* wrong," replied the Mentor. "You're focusing on performance and results. But that's only the tip of the iceberg. That's an end result—a destination. It's what you do to get there that really makes the difference. When you feel good about yourself, your performance will improve. But feeling good about yourself comes first."

"I feel like Tim," Jill agreed. "I'd like to be able to reassure myself all the time. But sometimes I need encouragement."

"You're looking for self-admiration," said the Mentor quietly.

Jill and Tim exchanged glances. *"Admiration?"* Tim exclaimed. "Isn't that a bit strong?"

"Sounds like self-flattery," said Jill.

"No." The Mentor shook his head. "It's entirely different. Self-admiration is fully deserved. It's the respect you give yourself for qualities that you truly possess." He settled back and looked at them. "It's okay to fail and it's okay to lose. However, it's *not* okay to see yourself as a failure or a loser. If you do, you set yourself up for a career of permanent self-doubt. A salesperson's potency comes from his principal weapon—and that's his sense of high self-worth.

"All of us have a personal set of standards from which we determine our worth. Outstanding salespeople have a great *appreciation* of that self-worth. You have to locate that source within yourself."

"But doesn't it really depend on how much you *know?*" asked Tim.

"Analysis, criticism, and caution you can get from anyone anytime—and they probably won't charge you for it," replied the Mentor. "But to reach your potential for success, you have to get beyond caution, fear of failing, and timidity. You can become a superachiever, but the spirit to realize that success must come from your heart. You are your own best advocate."

"Can you really tell whether a salesperson has the qualities that make for success?" asked Jill.

"Their presence tells the story. Effective sales professionals are intense, high-wattage people—not in the boisterous sense of the word, but relative to their own determination, drive, and passion.

"Regrettably, some salespeople are what I call spotlight-grabbing individuals. People like this are so enthralled by their sense of importance that they look for their names on the popularity polls. They may have talent, but talent is bogus unless it is converted into useful behaviors or positive customer actions.

"And then there's the opposite of that—individuals who are so self-deprecating that they're insecure in their relationships with others. These people are so timid and tentative that they don't create a noticeable, powerful presence; they would even go unnoticed in an empty room.

"They are like shadows: They leave no footprints in the snow. And they labor in obscurity a good bit of their careers."

"I'm sure that what you're saying is true. But how do I work toward the direction that's right for me?" Jill asked.

And that was when the Mentor outlined The Way to Self-Admiration.

## ✦✦✦ THE WAY ✦✦✦

✔ **Nurture your inner sense of worth.**

The first step toward empowering yourself is believing you *can*. Discover a confidence in yourself. You count for something; you make a difference. You are the single best option available to the customer.

✔ **Avoid self-defeating traps.**

If you are tentative and you have a shaky view of yourself, the customer will pick up on that and treat you as less important than you really are. Don't let that happen to you. Stick up for yourself. Claim your strengths and capitalize on these strengths day after day.

✔ **Send positive messages.**

A negative-energy person sends self-messages like, "I am not ready yet," or "I lack the skill," or "I am going to fail again." Replace those messages with positive self-messages like, "I count for something," "I will make a difference," "I am going to be great today." Be forever optimistic. People who thrive are never satisfied with just making it from day to day.

Remember, a self-confident attitude leads to superior performance.

✔ **Err on the side of generosity and graciousness.**

To be an effective salesperson, you have to be emotionally and interpersonally literate. You have to be able to say you *care* about the customer. Tear down the self-imposed barriers of self-centeredness. Always do more rather than less for the customer.

✔ **Improve your working image of yourself.**

There is a lot about you that is good—that the person you're trying to impress and influence doesn't even know about. Ask yourself, "What is getting in the way of my being my own best person?" Think of ways you can look better, think better, and act better. Make sure you put a blue ribbon on yourself.

✔ **Celebrate your uniqueness—your difference.**

A healthy sense of self-worth is the launchpad of success. It provides you with the personal energy and the grit to face emotional danger and get charged up with determination and resolve. Your belief in yourself will sustain you during the low moments you will encounter in selling.

✔ **Take time to appreciate and affirm your self-worth.**

Pick two positive attributes in yourself and hold them up for self-examination. For me this would be passion and determination. For you it could be something else—like courage, honesty, or enthusiasm. In any case, these are the rock-hard attributes that you will bring to others. When you know why people hold you in high regard, why they admire you, then the worth they see in you is transformable into conscious actions that will influence others.

✔ **Get excited about everything you do.**

Love your work: Demonstrate high energy and focused creativity. Strive to become a prominent symbol of change and productivity with your customers. Develop a restless appetite for success. Package yourself to be exciting: You can do this by painting your face with victory.

✔ **Warm up the January within yourself.**

No one can succeed if they are at odds with themselves. Don't spend time processing what you *don't* like about yourself. Rather, dwell on the things that you *do* like. Approach your selling activities with the eagerness of a racehorse that won't be denied the victory.

✔ **Continue to develop goals that will inspire you to achieve.**

Create a winning work style and adopt a winning mood. Set new sales standards that others will aspire to match. Perfection is not unrealistic: It is nothing more or less than doing the very best you can.

✦  ✦  ✦

"But isn't it risky to become *too* self-absorbed?" asked Jill.

"Self-absorption and self-admiration are two different things," the Mentor pointed out. "When salespeople are self-absorbed, they are so unconcerned about their customers' needs that they might as well be on another planet when they make a sales call."

"I'm sure there are ways to break out of self-absorption," Tim noted. "In fact, I'm always trying to find ways myself."

"Yes, there are ways," the Mentor agreed. "In fact, those ways are what I call *powering up*."

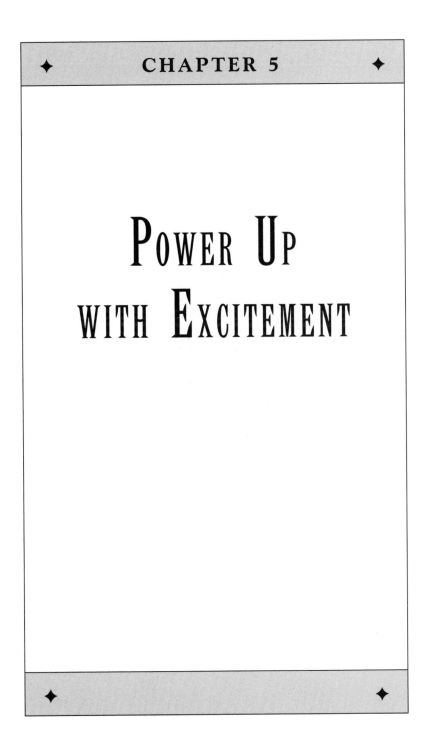

# CHAPTER 5

# POWER UP WITH EXCITEMENT

# The Key to Powering Up

*Passion is the magic that makes
impossible-to-meet goals possible.*

Every now and then, Tim caught Jill looking at the Mentor with a slightly quizzical expression on her face. Finally, the Mentor noticed, too.

"Was there something you wanted to ask?" he inquired.

"Well, yes, but—" Jill stopped, embarrassed, as though she had been caught staring at a stranger.

"Go ahead."

Jill sighed. "It's just that I was thinking how different you sound from—well, from some of the chronic complainers around this place."

Tim nodded. "A lot more positive, I'd say."

"Yes," Jill agreed. "But it's more than positivism. Some people don't have anything good to say about *anything*. People like that take the wind out of my sails."

"I can give you a good, easy hint about that one," the Mentor responded quickly. "Avoid them."

Tim shook his head. "Sometimes that's not easy to do.

They're looking for a sounding post. Someone to sympathize with them. They seem to know when you're down, and that's when they jump in to share their 'ain't-it-awfuls' with you."

"I call that Junk Talk. I assure you, great sales professionals don't listen to Junk Talk," said the Mentor. "It depletes their energy.

"You'll always run into a certain number of people who feel good by feeling bad," the Mentor continued. "The trouble is, their attitude is as lethal as a contagious disease. I guarantee you'll catch a disabling case of the blahs if you keep frequent company with them. Their bodies may be present, but for some of these people, their hearts left the job a long time ago.

"When these people are on the job, their thinking goes something like this:

'If it's bad, it will probably happen to me.'
'I don't want to be responsible if things go wrong.'
'It's too much trouble to get involved.'
'I don't get the kind of support I need.'
'What a pain this customer is!'
'This place is going to the dogs.'

"These souls carry briefcases full of fear, apprehension, and resentment from one customer meeting to the next. They can be seen tiptoeing into the customer's office, heads bowed, thinking the worst.

"Listening to chronic complainers like these will rob you of hope and dampen your spirits. When people reach an advanced stage of negativism, it's called the Poor-Me Syndrome. It keeps them *coping* rather than *influencing*. In other words, this kind of person is putting up with the negative situation rather than trying to do something positive to change it."

"But we *all* have things to complain about," said Jill. "Why should we pretend that problems don't exist?"

The Mentor reflected a moment. "I'll never deny that we face adversity. But I think complaining about it is more than a waste of time. It actually puts age on you. It shortens your stay on earth."

"But you've been doing this job for years—" Tim began.

"Decades, is more like it." The Mentor laughed. "And you're wondering how I deal with the troublesome stuff and manage to stay passionate about what I do?"

Tim nodded sheepishly.

"It's a day-to-day thing, Tim," the Mentor went on. "I have to consciously work at it every moment of the day."

"I keep trying to do that," Tim agreed. "But sometimes I feel totally exhausted and drained after a day of gut-wrenching calls. Is there a way to get passionate for every sales call, every time out, even if you've had a major-league bad day?"

"Yes, there is," said the Mentor. And then he explained.

## ✦✦✦ THE WAY ✦✦✦

✔ **Let success go to your head.**

Avoid worry. When you worry, you automatically picture the worst-case scenario. It's an energy-depleting activity that can result in a cynical, disheartened, and negative outlook on the sales call.

Let the momentum of the last good sales call propel you into the next one. Intensify your efforts and focus on the hope and excitement of your next great sales encounter.

✔ **Put on a confident sales face.**

Ingest a healthy dose of self-respect. Dwell upon positive experiences. That way, winning images are always fresh in your mind. Constantly recall those images when you walk into future sales engagements.

✔ **Keep the right company.**

Avoid people who, instead of highlighting your positives, take delight in pointing out your shortcomings or telling you how they could have done it better. Don't slow down to their speed. These are dangerous liaisons—keep a safe distance!

✔ **Have faith.**

Don't let disappointment straitjacket your ambition. If the last sales call was less than you wanted it to be, and you're feeling bitterness, anger, or lingering resentment, make sure you work through these feelings as rapidly as you can. Holding on to those emotions contaminates your ability to see the world positively. It floods your consciousness with negative thoughts that blind you to the great possibilities that exist in others. Look ahead to the next sales call, rather than dwelling on the pain and disappointment of the previous experience. Show a new readiness to create *anam cara* with your next customer.

Have faith that darkness and despair will give way to enlightenment and hope.

✔ **Use your passion as fuel.**

Convert negative energy into passion. Replace self-absorption with customer-centeredness, abruptness with thoughtfulness, impatience with tolerance, judgmentalism with influenceability, selfishness with generosity, negativity with optimism, timidity with courage, and despair with hope.

✦ ✦ ✦

"Haven't you left something out?" asked Jill.

"What?" The Mentor's eyebrows were raised quizzically.

"Well, some salespeople *try* to be passionate and get powered up, but there's something missing. They seem almost lifeless: They take an anemic approach to their sales activities."

"You know what's missing?" Tim interjected. "The drive for victory."

"I think you're right." The Mentor paused, reflecting. "To be successful, you must have drive and the unrelenting desire to succeed. When you have the will to win, all your past defeats just whet your appetite for victory."

"That's competitiveness," observed Tim.

"Exactly," replied the Mentor with a smile. "We can't do without it."

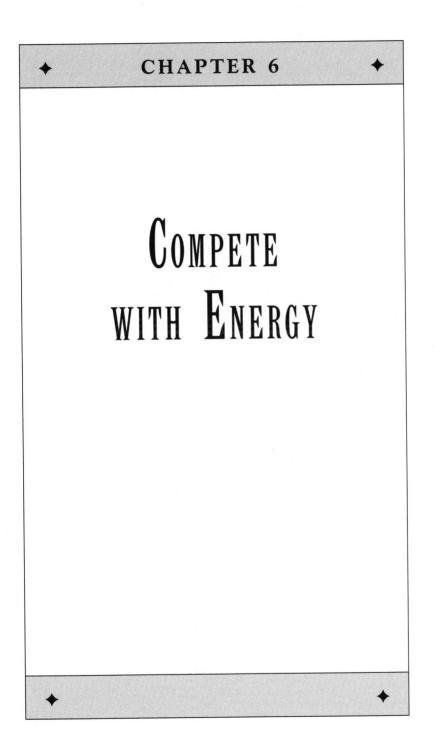

CHAPTER 6

# COMPETE
# WITH ENERGY

# The Key to Competitiveness and the Will to Win

*Competitiveness comes from the soul. It's a compelling desire to succeed. It's your ability to look down the barrel of a competitor's gun and not be intimidated but, rather, be motivated.*

"I always want to be a jump ahead of my competitors," Jill said, "but if I watch their every move, it seems like I'll always be playing catch-up."

"And of course that's an impossible situation," the Mentor agreed. He reflected a moment. "You know, it's not so much a case of facing down your competition. It's more like outperforming your competition. You have to decide to compete or retreat, and if you compete, it takes emotional toughness, unrelenting perseverance, and a will to endure until you are victorious.

"Unlike some competitive sports, where defense is so critical, the opposite is true in selling. Salespeople who just want to be as good as their competitors are underperformers. They play defensively, putting their energy into preventing their competition from gaining position rather than advancing the foothold they have worked so hard to achieve."

The Mentor thought a moment before continuing.

"When you consistently demonstrate a higher level of commitment to the customer, it's a sign of intense dedication."

"Dedication—" Jill seemed momentarily preoccupied with the word. "I've been trying to understand why I find myself thinking about my customers almost all the time—how to help them, what they need, what else I can do for them. I always thought it was sheer terror of losing the business."

"And all along you were just trying to beat out your competitor for the business." Tim laughed.

"That's definitely part of it," the Mentor agreed. "Still, I hope there aren't many people in our organization who think that's all it is," he added with a thoughtful look. "This state of mind is a trap. From what I've seen, it severely narrows your chances, because it limits your actions to doing only enough to get by your competitors rather than resolving your customers' needs."

"I look at the way some of my competitors are operating"—Jill shook her head—"I mean, it's frightening how much they can outresource me. I can't turn my back on what they're doing."

"I agree, you have to watch your competitors," responded the Mentor. "But that doesn't mean imitating them. I say, put your whole heart and soul into being *better*. The second you start to revere your competitor, you put yourself at a disadvantage. You have resigned yourself to a 'wannabe' mentality. That attitude puts you one down mentally and has you playing catch-up."

"But it seems like customers' requirements are escalating all the time," observed Jill.

"We've all remarked about how much smarter the customer is getting," the Mentor said. "It's my contention that this is really a benefit to you—because if you're any better than your competitor, your customer is smart enough that he will notice it."

"And now our competitors are getting smarter, too!" Tim lamented.

"Absolutely right," the Mentor agreed. "Count on it—if your competitor is any good, he will try his hardest to out-position you. You can be sure he will work harder, act more aggressively, and apply more pressure on the customer to dislodge you from the Promised Land. It's his job. And it's *your* job if the situation is reversed."

"You know, I used to be cordial and charming with competitors," Tim observed. "I figured we could at least shake hands and say it was a fair match. Now I'm not so sure I want to go out of my way to do this anymore."

"They'll all try to get information from us," Jill agreed. "I know that from experience now."

"Well, I'll tell you my policy—and this too comes with experience," the Mentor observed. "If your competitor ever asks you how you're doing, just tell him you're making a living. Let it go at that! Believe me, he doesn't need to know any more!"

Jill smiled. "And here we thought you were so mellow. Don't tell me you're so focused on winning!"

"It's an integral part of The Way," the Mentor observed. And then he continued.

# ✦✦✦ THE WAY ✦✦✦

✔ **Enjoy the will to win.**

That will should come from within—and not be simply a response to your competitors. Try winning because it's personally important to you. Remember, when you want the business more than your competitor does, you have a mental edge.

✔ **Take your competitor off the pedestal.**

Although you might be impressed by your competitor at first glance, don't be intimidated. You can have a healthy respect for him—but reverence? No! You don't have to kiss your competitor's ring. If you put your competitor above yourself or your company, you're playing catch-up.

✔ **Never back down from your competitor.**

Find your competitor's soft spot and outperform him. Your competitors are never out of the running. For this reason, *always* treat your customer like a prospect who could dismiss you in a moment. In that way you will constantly stay mentally focused on responding to the customer's needs and building the business.

✔ **Don't spend a lot of time looking over your shoulder.**

If you're basing your activity on how rapidly your competitor is catching up, that's defensive selling as well. Instead, look ahead and do concrete things for your customer that advance your position while putting distance between you and your competitor.

✔ **Rearrange the terrain.**

Don't compete on equal terms. Instead, set the standard. Do things better and do them more quickly. In the final analysis, you decide how awesome you are—and you decide whether you're really better than your competitor. Force your competitor to live up to *your* standards . . . if he can.

✔ **Be the comeback kid.**

Minimize your competitor's impact by doing something to reposition yourself. Treat any setback as temporary, and be determined to retake your lost sales position. Be inspired to get it back. Do something tangible to reposition yourself. Find a way to launch a fresh and creative initiative for your customer. Don't set yourself at a competitive disadvantage by taking it on the chin and not mounting a comeback effort.

✔ **Prevent disaster.**

Don't underestimate your opponent. Remember that the arrogance of success is the threshold of disaster! If your competitor is any good, he will mount a determined counteroffensive and launch a fierce assault. Expect it—and prepare for it!

✔ **Create a profile of endurance.**

The customer's inaction or delays shouldn't discourage you. Outdistance your opponent in pursuit of the business. You can always relax after you have won—but only for a brief moment. Be an Olympic-caliber long-distance runner. Remember that the race for the prize is not necessarily won by the fastest runner, but rather goes to the one who keeps on running past the finish line.

✔ **Wear your opponent down.**

Take an active stance in the customer relationship. A passive stance could turn out to be motivation for your competitor—and could inspire him to intensify his efforts and become a serious challenge. Your aggressiveness and resolve, on the other hand, could wear your opponent down, causing him to lose heart, undercommit his resources, and become a benign adversary who turns his attention in another direction. And that's just what you want.

✔ **Build on your position.**

Never take the business for granted. Listen to the users of your ideas and solutions. Enlist them in helping you find new ways to be a better resource, and build your position. Silence your opposition by providing concrete evidence of your devotion and value to the customer on a regular basis. This will demonstrate that you are constantly striving to earn the right to the business by helping him succeed and achieve his goals.

✔ **Outlast the will of your competitor.**

Once you have achieved the prize, treat it like a treasure that could be snatched away from you in the blink of an eye. Be determined to outpersevere and outperform your competitor for a long time.

✔ **Celebrate!**

If indeed you have surmounted your competitor's position, take a victory lap. Stand in the winner's circle. You deserve it. But get back on the track rapidly. Pass the good things on. Celebrate with pride and generosity by giving credit to your boss, your support team, your customer, your spouse and children, your significant other, your dry cleaner, the airport baggage handlers, your hairstylist—everyone! Pass it on.

✦  ✦  ✦

"I agree with everything you've said about competitiveness," mused Jill. "But still, there are times when I know I'm a noncontender for the business."

"*How* do you know?" Tim demanded. "People and needs change so rapidly, you could become a front-runner almost overnight."

"That's true," the Mentor agreed. "Your number may

come up sooner than you think." He reflected a moment. "But of course you can't stand passively by, waiting in the wings for something good to happen. In fact, I believe it's critical at all times to know where you stand with a customer. It's the essence of positioning."

"What do you mean by positioning?" asked Tim.

"As it relates to selling, position is your current status and degree of influence in the customer relationship."

"Well, you're either in good position or bad position—" Jill interjected.

"Or no position at all," Tim finished for her.

The Mentor smiled. "There's a little more to it than that. In all of our customer relations, we are either winning, losing, or holding on to position with customers. And position progression is the act of improving your position or status in the customer relationship. I use a position model as a tracking index—sort of a reference point. As you move through the stages of position, your objective is to draw ever closer to the inner circle."

"I'm not sure I understand." Jill wore a puzzled expression.

"I'll have to show you," replied the Mentor, searching for a pad in his desk drawer. He placed the pad on his blotter and without a moment's hesitation drew a number of concentric circles.

"I call it the Position Progression Model," he said.

# CHAPTER 7

# ACHIEVE PREFERRED POSITION

# The Key to Becoming the Only Choice

*The core objective of all selling activity is to reach the position of maximum effectiveness and profitability with your customers. It's called Preferred Position.*

J ill and Tim considered the four-ring diagram, while the Mentor carefully wrote words inside each of the rings. When the Mentor was done, the diagram looked like this:

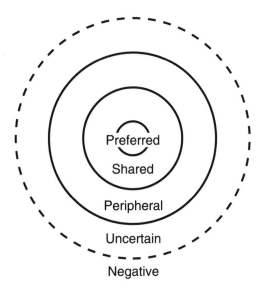

"Interesting," said Tim. "But how will this help us in selling?"

"Your position is your sales report card."

"What do you mean?" asked Tim.

"Well, one way to see the position model is as your circle of influence," rejoined the Mentor. "Understanding the model is the first step toward using it effectively: You have to see where you are in this model to help understand the quality and productivity of your current business relationship. But the Position Progression Model also helps you set personal objectives for all future sales activities. And this model provides a reference, so you can understand your competitive position in relation to the customer and your competition."

The Mentor thought a moment before he added, "There's another way this model helps, too: It provides further guidance, so you know what you have to do to advance your position. It enables you to be mission-ready.

"Positioning is your rank with the customer," he added. "It's the measurement of where you stand in your customer's eyes. Remember, the closer you are positioned to the inner circle, the more power you have to influence change and get things done."

Jill examined the diagram with a puzzled expression. "What's that mean?" she asked finally. Her finger was on the word "Negative."

"That's not really the beginning," the Mentor observed. "When you're in Negative Position, you've actually fallen out of favor. You're considered a nonresource. Perhaps you lost the account because of perceived deficiencies. Or you may have inherited a customer who views you negatively because your predecessor lost his grip, underperformed, and failed to retain the special-status relationship.

"Whatever the reason, the magic is gone when you fall to Negative Position. You've been set adrift. You've got low approval ratings, and you're really not considered reliable any longer. So you need to search for new and unique ways to rebuild the relationship and regain your lost position."

"And the rebuilding—that begins with Uncertain Position?" Tim asked.

The Mentor nodded. "With most customers, yes. When you have Uncertain Position, you're on the outside looking in. The account relationship may offer exciting opportunities—but nothing substantial is happening at this point, either because you just started calling on the customer or because the customer has gone through a change in command. A change of command could mean that your key contact has been replaced with another person you do not know much about. In the case of the replacement, you do not know very much about his special needs, nor does he fully understand your ability to provide value.

"But in either case you have the potential to improve your position. And the higher your position, the more power you have to accomplish your mission. So, expect to be kept at arm's length until you become a proven entity."

"It looks like a long distance from Uncertain to Preferred Position," Tim observed wryly, studying the model.

"It is"—the Mentor nodded—"but moving from one position level to another may not be an orderly process. You could find it to be a long march. Or you may be able to leapfrog ahead quickly—if you can get inside the customer's organization, expand your network, create an advocacy, and shift the balance of power in your direction by getting business away from your competition.

"Position progression represents growing dominance. But of course you can fall fast if there is a sudden and serious breakdown in your commitment."

Tim was gazing at the diagram. He pointed to the circle that was the next level up from Uncertain.

"Peripheral Position?" he queried, looking up at the Mentor. "I suppose that means you're calling on the customer, but you haven't secured any business."

"Or you *have* opened the account, but you're only getting the crumbs," the Mentor agreed. "When a salesperson is in Peripheral Position, he's fighting to have his voice heard. The customer begins to find out something about you. He gains a basic understanding of your organization's capabilities, while at the same time you have the chance to develop a solid understanding of the customer's special needs as they relate to what you represent. While you are in Peripheral Position, you begin to develop rapport with the customer's key people who one day soon will form your advocacy.

"In Peripheral Position you may get a shot at some of the business, but for the most part it will be a minimum amount."

"That's *exactly* where I am with several major customers," Jill observed. "The trouble is, I don't feel they're being completely open and candid with me."

The Mentor nodded. "That's one of the drawbacks of Peripheral Position, I'm afraid. That customer may be coming to you last—after going to your competitors first who are in Shared or Preferred Position. That customer is still viewing you out of the corner of his eye. You're on the fringe, with limited trust, limited access to key customers, and not much influence. In essence, in Peripheral Position you're being tested—examined under the microscope. To win a larger share of the business, you have to outperform your competitor when given a chance. In Peripheral Position you not only have to survive the test, but you must also pass the test with flying colors."

"Then what's the difference when you move into Shared Position?" Jill inquired. "I mean, how will I *know* I've advanced in the customer's standing?"

"It's been my experience that you can feel a change in the relationship climate," responded the Mentor. "There's a significant warming. When you're in Shared Position, you're one of several valued resources, with a significant amount of business and the potential for increasing it. You'll find that you've won considerable trust from the customer, and even though you have limited influence, it's significant."

"I think I know one sure sign of Shared Position," Jill interjected.

"What's that?" asked the Mentor.

"When you can force your competitors to do something that you do better."

"I don't get it," said Tim.

"Well, if your competitors have to meet *your* standards, that means you're a superior among equals," said Jill. "The customer is measuring you against others. But you have the edge."

"That's right," agreed the Mentor. "You're literally sharing the same arena."

"I'll bet price becomes an important factor when you're in Shared Position," Tim observed.

"Certainly, price—and a lot of other factors as well," the Mentor concurred. "As your business share increases, you can definitely expect your competitor to work hard to hold on to his business while at the same time going after the business you have now."

"And if the reverse is true?" asked Jill. "What if you wind up taking business from your competitor, and *you* become the dominant resource?"

"Well, in that case—" The Mentor smiled. "In that case you're no longer a *resource*—you're *the source*."

"Preferred Position," Jill guessed.

"Exactly."

"I *want* it," said Tim.

"You should," the Mentor confirmed with a smile. "In selling, Preferred Position is the Promised Land. When you're there, you have the majority of the customer's business, or you have all of the profitable business you want." He pointed to the center of the diagram. "In Preferred Position you have preeminent status—the complete trust of the customer, easy access to vital information, strong advocates who sing your praises, and extensive influence.

"In Preferred Position you have what I call 'walking rights.' No door is closed to you. The customer comes to you first because you're the person of choice. You are a trusted individual—a known quantity—and you set the standards by which your competitors are judged."

"You make it sound like an invulnerable position," said Tim.

"Far from it." The Mentor shook his head. "It's true,

you're at center stage—but the demands are intense. If you lapse into a state of total security, you may find that you're out of position in two shakes of a lamb's tail.

"To remain in Preferred Position requires a high degree of vigilance. Because you're the primary source of ideas and information, you always need to look for new and different ways to help your customer succeed and achieve, using your recommendations and solutions.

"You need to take extra precautions to insulate yourself from competitive activity—especially because the customer may begin to feel vulnerable having all or most of his business under one roof. You have to do the job so well for the customer that you never have to look over your shoulder.

"But if you let someone down who's counting on you while you're in Preferred Position, you may go into free fall from Preferred to Negative Position—depending on the gravity of the circumstance. The penalties for non-performance could be severe. Gross inaction will cause the customer's patience and tolerance to wear thin—and if your position slips, you will receive a very clear and concise message: You will not get as much repeat business as you are used to."

The Mentor drew a vertical line from the center of the Position Progression Model to the word "Negative" outside all the circles.

"If you fall toward Negative Position," the Mentor observed, "there will be a lot of finger-pointing during your descent—accompanied by widespread rumblings of discontent."

"It's all so simple." Tim shrugged. "All you have to do is get to Preferred Position—and stay there."

"Sure." The Mentor smiled. "That's all."

"Is there a secret to all this?" asked Jill, looking from Tim to the Mentor.

"No, no great secret," replied the Mentor. It was only after a thoughtful moment that he added, "But there is a Way."

# ✦✦✦ THE WAY ✦✦✦

✔ **Treat the customer like a prospect.**

Remember that to retain Preferred Position, it takes extensive precall planning, flawless execution, and relentless follow-through. Stay on watch. Never, ever take the customer for granted, because if you do, your rival won't. Be vigilant and be on guard. Never let up, once you've reached Preferred Position. If anything, increase your level of intensity. Remember, there is no permanent safety in Preferred Position. Treat the customer like a prospect you're forever trying to win over to your side.

✔ **Find out what matters.**

Position is a vertical climb that can be a long odyssey with lots of hazardous obstructions along the way. Indispensable to accessing the center of influence is understanding your customer's business needs. This will help you get a clear fix on the customer's critical concerns as they relate to your solution capabilities and put you in a position to respond with a recommendation.

✔ **Build a strong advocacy.**

You cannot make it to the top and stay there if the customer's people don't want you there. To make it to Shared or Preferred Position, you must broaden and deepen your relationship with all of the support players in the customer's organization.

Don't overlook the other people who have helped you get there and who will continue to help you stay in Preferred Position. Talk to them, work with them, credit them with your success, and above all, treat them with respect.

Take their guidance seriously and always make them feel important and needed. Remember, when you are fighting it out for Preferred Position, you want everybody cosponsoring you and cheering you on.

✔ **Respond to the turn of events.**

Keep your eyes wide open and your ears acutely tuned, so you'll always know what's going on and what's coming down. Step to the head of the class by reading and rereading your customer's annual report. Implement the actions that will support your customer's strategic plan. Remember, it is a blueprint of how they plan to operate in the future!

Knowing your customer's strategic direction will

provide the guidance you need to respond to a turn of events. Really brilliant business professionals understand the strategic plan, vision, mission, and operating values better than most of the people inside the customer's organization. Be a step ahead, and you will never be too slow in responding to the customer's new and changing needs.

✔ **Be vigilant.**

Always audit your status in the relationship. Find out how your recommendations and solutions are performing. A failure to be constantly vigilant and attentive to correcting performance deficiencies will weaken your position and sharply alter the customer's view of you as a reliable resource. Gross inaction will cause the customer's patience and tolerance to wear thin. If you're smart, you will see it coming. That being the case, stop the slippage. Strengthen your hold on the business. Do something—do anything—to get yourself back on firm footing.

✔ **Upgrade your position.**

Avoid complacency. Never settle for the status quo. Maintaining the status quo is an investment in mediocrity. It could cause you to be dismissed for negligence, and it is an open invitation to an unwanted guest—your competitor.

Constantly look for new and unique ways to keep the relationship fresh, vital, and advancing.

This will insulate you from vigorous competitive advances and enable you to move your position upward. Always look for a better way to serve your customer.

 **Love 'em all!**

Avoid being labeled as "his boy" or "her girl." If some people see you favoring other people, they will resent this and take a tough line against your ideas. That's the best way to send you the signal that they want you to pay attention to them. Go out of your way to make everyone feel special and vital to your success.

**Marshal your forces.**

The customer will find out what kind of power and influence you have by the way your support team handles his business in the long term. For this reason, encourage your internal service support professionals to bend over backward for your customer every time out. Sell them on how vital he is to your business.

Point out the customer's value to each member of your team. Treat your internal support team like valued customers by always thanking them on the great job they are doing on your behalf. This will keep your team committed to the customer's special needs and help you tighten your hold on the business while advancing your privileged status.

✦ ✦ ✦

"May I copy that?" Jill asked, indicating the drawing of the Position Progression Model.

"Of course." The Mentor smiled. He tore off the top sheet from the pad and handed it to her.

"You know," said Tim, "when I first looked at that model, it seemed like a target with a bull's-eye in the center. But as you were talking about it, I realized it's really the customer at the center of those circles. All our sales activities have a single focus—moving closer to that customer."

"Yes," agreed the Mentor. "Creating intimacy or *anam cara* with the customer is the foundation message in all selling. Because you have the power to influence, you ultimately upgrade your position. You are poised for future growth.

"And it's essential if you are going to improve your position. If you're out of sight and out of mind, you're out of position."

"I'm wondering something." Jill paused.

"Ask," urged the Mentor.

"Of all the things you've told us—everything that we need to achieve Preferred Position—what would you say is the *most* essential?"

"A tough question," the Mentor responded. After a moment's hesitation, he added, "Obviously, you need to have many abilities. And perhaps one of the most important is being able to listen."

"Why is that so important?" asked Tim.

"Every time you listen—really listen—to the customer,"

responded the Mentor, "it's the same as saying, 'I am interested, I care, and I really want to help.' When the customer believes you really do, then you have increased your power and ability to influence."

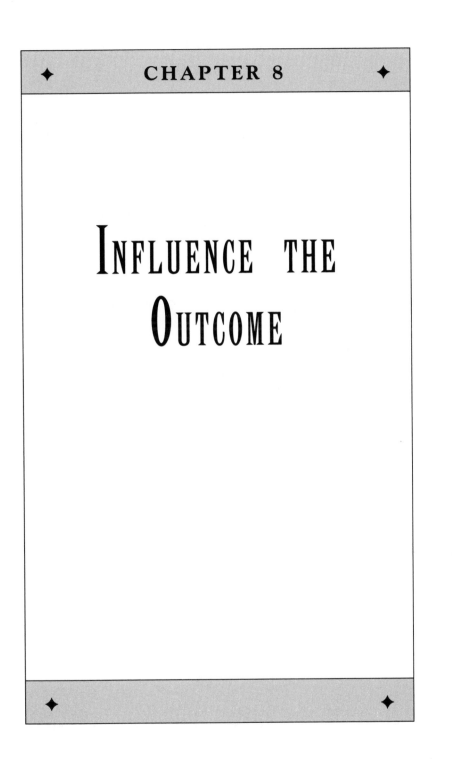

CHAPTER 8

# INFLUENCE THE OUTCOME

# The Key to Influencing

*If your spirit is missing from the meeting, your sales call will deteriorate into a conversation of good intent.*

"Some people think that if you have the gift of gab, you'll be a great salesperson," said the Mentor. "But this is not necessarily so. My Irish mother used to refer to this type of person as a Gobahon—a person who has a lot to say but doesn't say much. Consequently, a Gobahon is not taken seriously in some cases—and ultimately has no impact on events. Influencing, on the other hand, is a process that gives you an activity destination."

The Mentor paused a moment, considering his words before he continued. "Influencing is a road map that will take you to where you want to be. It's the process of transferring your conviction and passion to another person so that he acts on your recommendation."

Jill looked chagrined. "I never really thought about influencing in those terms. I don't really have *any* road map for my sales calls. I mean, I get mentally ready for every call. But planning what I'm going to do—that's something else."

"What do you recommend?" Tim asked the Mentor. "How do I avoid being viewed as a Gobahon? Are there any hard and fast rules that will help us make better sales calls?"

"In response to your question, let me say that I've seen three kinds of salespeople in my career," the Mentor replied. "One reacts purely on instinct. He does minimal preparation and hopes that he'll win the business by using his intuition and his powers of persuasion.

"The other kind of salesperson clearly knows his objectives and how to achieve them—but once he has a plan, he holds to it rigidly and uncompromisingly.

"The third type goes into a sales situation fully prepared—with thoroughly outlined plans and objectives—but at the same time, he has the flexibility to modify and adjust. He can change the strategy in midcourse or even midsentence if it's not working."

"Well, it's only common sense to be the third type," observed Jill.

"Yes," replied the Mentor. "But while it's common sense, it's not common practice. The third person I've just described has a great power in his hands—the power to *influence*."

"But how do you prepare to use that power?" asked Jill.

"Maybe I should tell you how *not* to be prepared," the Mentor reflected, a far-off look in his eye.

"It seems like you are always prepared," said Jill.

"Not when I first started," mused the Mentor. "I remember when I used to muddle along. Confused and unfocused, I would stumble through the sales call, hoping I would do or say the right things. I made content-free, unpredictable sales calls. I was out of control, and I knew it. Many times, my sales calls started off well but lost steam and came apart at the seams."

"Sometimes I fear I'll always be stuck at that level," said Tim. "I feel like my sales presentations are like kernels of corn in a popcorn machine. They flip in a thousand different directions."

Jill laughed in recognition.

"Some sales calls are talkathons—a lot of words are exchanged, but with no substance," the Mentor agreed. "I recall I was so suited up with the armor of enthusiasm, I would attack the customer with unrelenting bursts of benefit statements. I just hoped something I said would tickle his fancy and hit the mark. Instead, a lot of my sales calls were long strings of conversation that ended up going nowhere." He shook his head. "It was only later on that my optimism dissolved into fear and caution."

"What changed it for you?" asked Jill.

The Mentor thought only a moment before he uttered a single phrase: "Listening and paying attention to what's important to the customer."

"But I think I do listen and pay attention," said Tim.

"Do you really hear your customer?" the Mentor wondered aloud. "Can you separate his voice from the background noise?"

"What do you mean?"

"Well, listening is like living by a large highway. The noise is continuous, but you don't hear it unless you deliberately listen to it. The same is true in selling. You really don't discover what the customer wants until you deliberately listen to him.

"If you don't really understand what's important to the customer, preparing your sales proposal will be as futile as mowing your lawn at midnight. You will not know where you've been or where you are going. You will be inviting stiff resistance to your solution because you didn't give the customer a role in helping you discover the problem. Only when you understand your customer's needs will you be in a position to resolve the customer's problem and ultimately win the business."

For an instant, Tim had a recollection of his last sales call—when he had given the clearest presentation of his career, only to be greeted by a cold, indifferent reaction from the customer.

"I never thought of listening as an avenue to influencing," observed Tim. "But I agree with the way you describe it. I don't see how anyone can influence unless they fully understand the customer's needs."

"That's the crux of it," said the Mentor. "That's how you become an *influencer*, a person who accurately sizes up the situation and can develop and deliver a commitment-inducing sales proposal that positions you as the only choice."

"I just realized something." Jill turned to the Mentor. "I've been using a hit-or-miss strategy!" She sounded almost astonished. "Do you know what I mean? My whole approach has been preaching and teaching. I've never really utilized listening—not to the degree you speak of—and I'll bet many of my recommendations have never really hit the mark. Sure, I ask some questions, but most of the time, I'm too preoccupied figuring out what I'm going to say, rather than listening to the customer's answers."

"You're not the only one," Tim agreed.

"Then let me show you another way," said the Mentor.

## ✦✦✦ THE WAY ✦✦✦

✔ **Become a vital component of your customer's enterprise.**

Learn your customer's business from top to bottom. Do this by getting the customer to tell you about his vision for the future. In so doing, the customer will tell you what his enterprise stands for, why it exists—and what the organization aspires to become. With this knowledge, you will be able to match your abilities to your customer's needs. You will be in a position to support your customer in the attainment of his aspirations.

Be sure to tell the customer what you stand for, your purpose, and how your future is connected to his company's future. In doing this, you will be creating a healthy level of intimacy and the beginning stages of *anam cara*. You will be in a better position to influence the decision-making process from the very outset.

✔ **Press flesh early and often.**

Get out from behind your computer screen, away from portable phone and fax machine. Make eyeball-to-eyeball contact with the customer. Remember the old adage "Out of sight—out of mind—out of consideration."

Avoid carrying on long-distance relationships. They're for the birds—and, besides, they're no fun. It takes the human factor out of selling. Don't be a figment of your customer's imagination while your competitor is camped out on his doorstep, making hay while the sun shines in your absence. Frequency of contact is a strong bonding strategy and creates an obligation on the part of the customer to take you seriously. Your ability to influence the customer will be greatly multiplied by your physical presence. Be there, shaking hands, early and often.

✔ **Get "mission-ready" for every sales call.**

Take luck, wishful thinking, and groping-and-hoping out of your efforts to influence people and gain the business. View every sales call as a high-stakes engagement that you prepare for. Avoid a hastily fashioned sales call that has an ambiguous objective accompanied by a fuzzy plan of action. Make your objective clear, your strategy creative, and your action steps concrete and doable.

✔ **Set a positive tone.**

You set the tone at the outset of all your sales engagements. Your personal actions at the beginning of the customer meeting will determine the events that follow. Get up for the sales call. Avoid the deadly combination of being a nonplussed salesperson with an uninspired customer. In this situation, nothing happens. The meeting becomes a big yawn, and any chance to improve your sales position flies out the door.

Capture your customer's attention and keep it. Let your customer experience and feel your passion. Instill your conviction into the customer's consciousness.

✔ **Prepare to win every vote.**

Bring everyone in on your game plan. There is no such thing as a swing vote, because if someone is against you, that person will sell the others on why they shouldn't do business with you. This could cause a decision delay and open up a bundle of nasty surprises—that is, your customer inviting additional competitors to present their qualifications.

✔ **Play the field.**

Avoid playing favorites. Becoming "his boy" is exclusionary and could cause petty jealousies that would drive a wedge between you and a customer's commitment to give you the business. Remember, the customer is *everyone* when you're on the customer's turf—and it's vital that you build warm and genuine positive contact with everyone you meet and go out of your way to meet.

Some of your customers' personnel have an imaginary sign reading "No Contact, Please!" That message is telegraphed to you in the form of a blank stare, a gaze that never meets your eyes. But you *can* get around the sign.

A salesperson who limits his contacts to a few people who are easy to meet is shutting the door on the possibility of relationships with others in the customer's organization. And those others could eventually become members of the vendor selection team as well as decision-influencers or decision-makers. Get *everyone* involved and beating the drum for you from the start. Strive to have everyone on your side—becoming advocates of your sales proposal.

✔ **Always walk in with a new idea in your head.**

When you show up, you are already giving something of value if the customer is listening to you. Don't make sales calls to see how things are going. An unplanned sales call is a sales call not worth making. Put teeth into all of your calls.

✔ **Stay engaged and centered.**

Concentrate on what is happening during the sales call. Meet the challenge; stay in the intensity of the moment. Free yourself from distractions that will cause your attention to shift. Don't break contact with the moment.

✔ **Know when to call it a day.**

It is better to deselect a customer rather than follow the customer into dangerous and unprofitable waters. Don't let the customer dictate the terms and conditions of the sale. This must be a collaborative effort, and it's got to be a good deal for everyone if it's going to work for the long term.

✦  ✦  ✦

"I know I can influence my customers to seriously consider my recommendation," said Tim. "But how do I arrive at a solution that's exactly right for them?"

"You won't get there by using seize, occupy, and defense tactics," the Mentor pointed out. "If you're going to understand The Way, I need to tell you about the two major strategies in influencing—discovery and resolution.

"In the discovery process, you are actively exploring your customer's needs. In resolution, you are passionately presenting your solution and asking for a commitment to action."

"That's *gold*!" said Tim.

"Once you've mastered it—yes," the Mentor agreed with a smile.

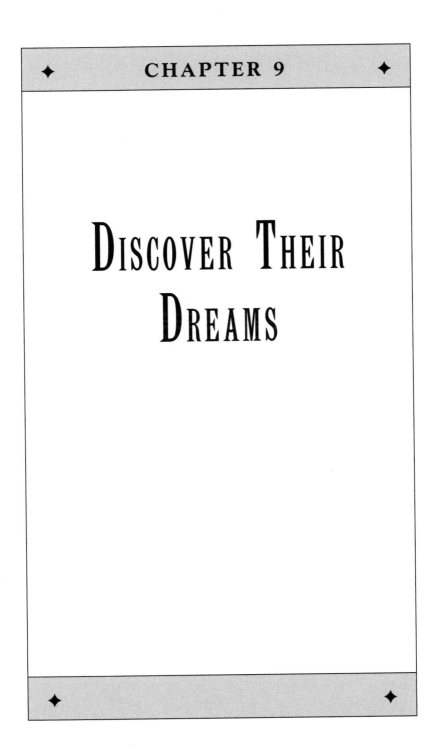

# CHAPTER 9

# DISCOVER THEIR DREAMS

# The Key to Discovery

*Asking high-return questions and listening to the customer's response is an advanced form of communication. It's the most important step in responding to the customer's call for help.*

The Mentor burst into a fit of laughter—a rare occurrence up to this point.

It was a moment before he explained. "You know, when I first started selling, I was guilty of carpet-bombing my customers with benefits, hoping that I would cover the problem with a million shots at the target. I would be so captivated by my own belief and passion that I would overlook understanding the customer's point of view. I was so in love with my own conclusions that it really didn't matter what needs the customer had.

"Little did I know that *discovery*—in the form of thought-provoking questions—would help me put my finger on the customer's nerve center and help me find out what really matters."

"Discovery!" Jill pounced on that word as if it held a special fascination for her. "I'd like to know more about the discovery process," she urged. "That's where I often have the most trouble. Some of my customers seem determined to remain mysterious. But I know I can't help them unless I know more about them and what they are trying to do to improve their organizations."

"What you're discovering is that good intentions will only get you so far," the Mentor observed.

Jill nodded. "I think I *rely* on good intentions to get the customer's interest," she said.

"You will get and hold your customer's interest in you by staying in *his* operating reality or area of interest," observed the Mentor. "In his mind the customer is asking, 'Will you go to bat for me with your organization?' and 'Will you deliver on commitments?' "

"I can think of some other things, too," Tim added. I know my customers are asking themselves, 'Can I rely on you?', 'Will I like working with you?', 'Can I trust what you tell me?', 'Can I trust you to learn all you can about my needs?' "

"If we don't answer those questions, the customer will never feel comfortable with us," Jill observed.

"I think you're right," said the Mentor. "But you tell the customer a lot about yourself with the questions that *you* ask."

"I'm not sure I follow," said Tim.

"Well, how would you feel about a doctor who prescribed medication before doing a careful and thorough diagnosis? What would you think of an attorney who pursued some legal action without first determining the facts? Similarly, salespeople who recommend a course of action to the customer without understanding the customer's needs are, in a way, guilty of dereliction of duty.

"Salespeople who do not listen to understand the customer's point of view are part of the problem—not the solution," the Mentor continued. "You might as well be a hollow voice crying out in the wilderness. Just as a patient will suffer if his doctor doesn't perform a complete and accurate diagnosis of the illness—and the person with a legal problem will have a weak case if his lawyer doesn't perform with due diligence—the customer's problem will go unsolved if you don't understand the problem to begin with.

"For the salesperson, good front-end discovery reduces guesswork and, ultimately, legwork," the Mentor went on. "What you don't do on the front end, you will wind up paying for on the back end. Your sales proposal will not respond to your customer's needs, and there will be no business coming your way."

The Mentor paused thoughtfully for a moment before continuing. "If you make a solution-based presentation without a careful exploration of the customer's needs at the front end of your sales effort, it's like putting the caboose before the steam engine. That's why discovery must always come before resolution.

"For this reason, you need to do deep work—which means a scholarly examination of the issues surrounding the customer's unresolved problems. When you do 'due diligence'—when it comes time to solve the customer's problems—you speak with authority."

"But what if you get more information than you need?" asked Jill.

"Does that ever happen?" Tim wondered aloud.

The Mentor shook his head. "Not in my view. The political realities of all business enterprises suggest that you can never have enough information. Information is your lifeline."

He settled back, taking in Jill and Tim with his steady gaze. "Discovery is your *entry point* into the relationship," said the Mentor. "It's your principal agenda. And the central questions in the discovery process are these: Did you find out what really matters? and Can you make things better for the customer?"

The Mentor reflected a moment before adding, "Of course, you *can* make things better. But you have to know The Way."

# ✦✦✦ THE WAY ✦✦✦

✔ **Be target smart.**

Make contact, and build a relationship with all of the decision-influencers. Find out how influential each person is by getting the answers to two important questions: "In what ways will you be involved in the decision-making process?" followed by, "What critical needs will I have to resolve in order to help you achieve your goals?"

✔ **Find a strategic partner.**

This person is the vital connection in the customer's organization who can help you identify and connect with current and future sales opportunities. Your strategic partner will manage you through the twists and turns and help you avoid the land mines.

He will make sure that you connect with all of the right people in all of the right places.

This individual can update you on how you are progressing as well as provide you with critical competitive intelligence. Your strategic partner is an advocate and a navigator all rolled into one.

✔ **Due diligence comes first.**

If you want to influence the customer to make a decision in favor of you, you must do your discovery in the form of due diligence. If you don't, you're involved in a guessing game. You will be asking the customer to make a leap of faith. Your selling statements will miss the mark.

✔ **Avoid ill-timed, ill-chosen questions.**

Don't ask the kinds of questions you should have answers to before you grace the customer's doorstep. They demonstrate shallow precall research and imply a lack of interest. Invest time in research and preparation before you make contact. In this way you will come across as informed, interested, and serious about the customer's business.

✔ **Find the Gap.**

Ask diplomatic, high-return questions that stimulate excitement and intrigue. For example: "What unique challenges is your business currently experiencing?", "What demands are your customers placing on you that they haven't in the past?", and "In what ways are you responding to the current economic environment?" With carefully crafted, high-return questions and keen observations, you will be locating the area of opportunity.

The area of opportunity is the gap that exists between what the customer really needs to happen and the actual situation he finds himself in. The Gap is your opening—it's your target. Once you have found the Gap, you have entered into the customer's operating reality—and that's where you always want to be.

✔ **Always thank the customer for information shared with you.**

It demonstrates gratitude for the customer's help, and it puts the customer at ease. This builds trust, promotes openness, and paves the way for you to secure more information.

✔ **Restate and verify your understanding.**

"In other words, what you are saying is . . ." "Is my understanding complete and accurate?" Questions like this help you arrive at a deep discovery. Arriving at an agreed-to need creates a shared view and lays the groundwork for your sales proposal. Remember, depth-based questions will get the customer involved in helping you find a solution, while at the same time creating respect for you as a heads-up business professional.

✔ **Be like a vacuum cleaner.**

Be quick to grasp all the information you can get your hands on. Try to read your customer's mind and picture the things the customer is thinking of. Understand the whole picture—not just part of it. Use the eyes in the back of your head, so you can "see" unspoken conversation—so you hear what the people on the other side of the wall are saying about their needs. A total and accurate assessment of the customer's situation will add to the firmness of your conviction when you present your solution.

✔ **Avoid the danger zone.**

You won't help the discovery process by exposing the customer's deficiencies in an embarrassing manner. You can't tell a mother that her baby is ugly—and you can't tell your customer that what he is doing is all wrong. It's a death trap. If your customer is proud of a solution he helped your competitor create and implement, acknowledge it—don't attack it. An acknowledgment, in this case, is an investment in the relationships bank.

✔ **Take the customer's concerns seriously.**

If you make the customer feel appreciated, listened to, taken seriously, and valued, that may be all it takes to sell your ideas. Make the customer a cocreator of the solution.

✔ **Put your finger on the nerve center.**

Don't let exploring the customer's needs become a low-key, passive part of your discussions. Get excited while the customer is telling you about his dreams. This activates the spirit of inclusiveness. If you become excited about your customer's short-term and long-term needs, you are getting him to help you shape the solution.

✦ ✦ ✦

"Then it's absolutely essential to stay focused on the discovery process until it's complete," said Jill.

"You put your finger on it," replied the Mentor. "From listening comes wisdom; from speaking comes repentance. If you don't have the stomach for exploring the customer's needs, then you will always be a hit-or-miss salesperson. You will be regretting and repenting on a regular basis because your performance will be less than passable. Have the patience and restraint to sit on your solution until the appropriate time."

"When *is* the appropriate time?" asked Tim.

"I think you'll know when you're ready to move toward resolution," replied the Mentor. "That's the second part of influencing. It's when you're ready to present a benefit-saturated sales presentation that resolves the customer's needs. It's a podium moment!"

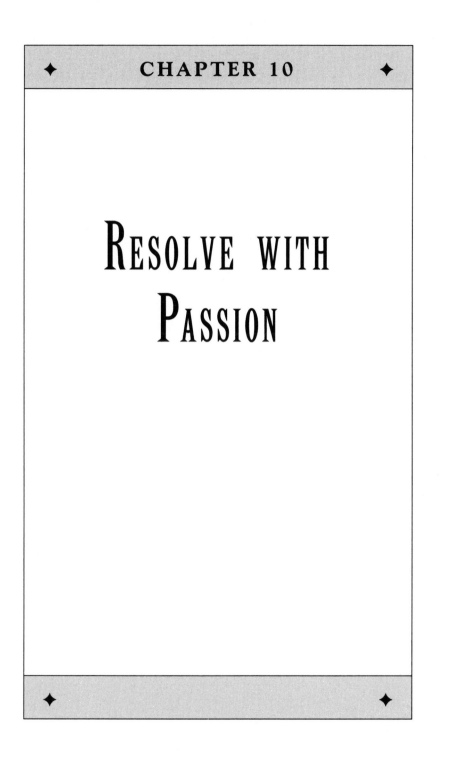

**CHAPTER 10**

# RESOLVE WITH PASSION

# The Key to Resolution

*Make sure the customer feels your heart when you make your sales presentation. The customer will pay for your passion, because it is, after all, the best thing you have to sell.*

"**P**assionately presenting your benefits is the key," the Mentor reflected. "And presenting your benefits passionately is spirit-lifting."

"I've read everything I can find about how to make a sales presentation," said Jill, "and I feel like I'm thoroughly prepared. But when I'm finally eyeball-to-eyeball with the customers, I'm not sure I'm influencing them at all. I'm making what I think are strong points—and they're pretending to listen—but then their eyes glaze over and I'm not sure where the presentation is going."

"Maybe they're convinced but not persuaded," said the Mentor.

"What's the difference?" asked Jill.

"Well, the customer may know he has a problem, but you need to *excite* him into taking action. You must be able to highlight the important differences between your recommen-

---

dation and that of your rival. It's called Resolving the Customer's Problem."

"That's exactly what I need to learn," said Tim. "You know, I really am convinced I'm bringing concrete value to the table. But my competitors are getting the business too often. And it's not necessarily because of a lower price or more favorable terms and conditions of sales."

The Mentor leaned back in his chair, tented his fingers, and gestured to the impressive pile of successfully sold sales proposals on the corner of his desk.

"You know, I've known of technical masters who had their proposal presentations down cold but who were DOA—dead on arrival. They're solemn, humorless, dispassionate. They suffer from an acute case of dullness. Salespeople who make presentations in a lecturing, matter-of-fact tone are tedious and uninteresting to listen to. And it's because they lack passion. Their sales calls sound like the drone of a bumblebee."

"But I have the opposite kind of problem," Jill said. "Before a major sales presentation, I typically spend a sleepless night of anticipation. I become so intense, I spend the morning before the presentation in the antacid aisle of the nearest convenience store."

"That's taking it a little too far." The Mentor laughed. "But I think you'd agree, we all face a challenge—to design and deliver a sales presentation that educates, excites, and inspires the customer to take action. To do this, you have to be passionate about your solution to the customer's problem. After all, it is your passion that brings your conviction and dedication out in the open for the customer to see. To me, anything less than a passionate presentation is a low-intensity event at a superficial level of interaction. If you do not believe deeply in your plan to solve the customer's problem, you will sound shallow. You will have the words, but the music will be missing.

"When customers get up in the morning, I assure you they don't necessarily start the day by thinking about you, your product and services. However, when they go to bed that night, you want them so switched on that they're *only* thinking about you and your solution.

"When you make your sales presentation, you have to resonate and create an extraordinary moment. Your performance must be masterful. Your presentation has to be a stellar event that commands the customer's attention and holds it. In some sense your sales presentation requires an evangelist spirit. That's what passion is."

Tim felt shaken by the powerful sense of conviction in the Mentor's words—as if the Mentor himself were compelled to demonstrate the passion that he described.

"Design your presentation so it motivates the customer to take action *instantly*," the Mentor went on, his voice rising. "Remember, the customer will *pay* for your passion. And that's because what's in your passion is a promise of better things to come."

"But—what you're talking about—there's no way anyone can *fake* that," Jill protested.

"That's right," the Mentor replied instantly. "You have to be *absolutely convinced* that you're recommending the best course of action possible if you are going to be passionately convincing."

"And how do you know that?" asked Tim.

"I can't create the passion for you," said the Mentor. "Only you are capable of that." He reflected a moment. "But perhaps I can give you some guiding principles."

And the Mentor began.

## ✦✦✦ THE WAY ✦✦✦

✔ **Turn on the lights.**

When you walk into the room, you want the lights to go on. It's your energy that you want to use to provide the power. Package yourself to be exciting. Be poised and ready. Give your audience the feeling that they are in for a unique experience. A well-executed sales presentation puts you in the spotlight. Be the genuine article. Put your heart into it. Using positive body language, you will inspire your audience with your conviction.

✔ **Together is better.**

If the success of your presentation is in the hands of others, you owe it to yourself to make sure they have their parts down cold. If it's your customer, you have the ultimate responsibility for making sure the presentation is superb. Don't let anybody spoil it for you. Always make sure your copresenters are thoroughly checked out and well rehearsed. A well-rehearsed team can be an awesome force and give you a going-in advantage.

✔ **Be fully present during the entire sales call.**

For some salespeople, a sales call is thirty minutes of low-intensity chitchat. You don't create a sense of obligation on the part of your customer just by showing up. You have to *perform* while you're there if you want to obligate the customer to take you more seriously. If your spirit is absent, your sales call will deteriorate to a conversation of good intent.

✔ **Build energy and excitement in yourself.**

If you can't feel excitement in presenting your solution, you probably shouldn't be there. If you can't get excited about what you are selling, how can anybody else?

Use the presentation to your customer to demonstrate your passion for what you're selling. If you understand the other person's needs thoroughly— and if you are one hundred percent convinced that your solution will resolve their problem—you owe it to them to get them to do something about it. Any less from you is not operating in the customer's best interest.

✔ **Be a character that people don't want to stop talking about.**

Remember that you will always be measured against your competitor's accomplishments and personal stature. For this reason you want your unique presence to continue to occupy space in the customer's office long after you are gone. Look better than your competitor from the outset—not only in terms of the clothes you wear and the literature you distribute, but also in the way you prepare your presentation. An old friend of mine put it this way: "I'd rather stink than not smell at all." So take a risk and create a memorable moment that people will talk about for years to come. Outshine your competitor.

✔ **Avoid dead time.**

Dead time in the presentation is when you're giving a prolonged litany of product or service characteristics that are not connected to the customer's identified needs. It's a low-energy space in the presentation process that causes a customer's concentration to float. Remember that you earned the right to become an influential voice in resolving the customer's critical needs because you took the time to find out what they were. Always stay focused on the value you bring to the customer in the form of benefits. Come back to benefits over and over again.

✔ **Make the customer's heart beat faster.**

Communicate the value of your ideas, solutions, and recommendations through motivational statements. Remember, benefits make it easy for the customer to understand the full value of what you're selling.

Make your words count. Words are everything. They convey excitement, energy, and passion. Choose the most exciting word combinations to spotlight your benefits. When you are presenting your solution to the customer, your words should have impact. Use *exciting* language to inspire confidence in your solution. "Increased profits," "increased customer satisfaction," "more sales," "improved market share," "greater efficiency," "reduced cost," "reduced hassle," "less trouble," "greater sense of well-being," and "more productivity" are the word combinations that make the presentation of your benefits worthy of the customer's uninterrupted attention.

✔ **Develop a focused plan of action.**

Consider the following steps for making your presentation:

◆ *Positive Contact:* Create an atmosphere of excitement, curiosity, and openness. Start with a positive greeting in a tone that is upbeat and animated. Give your customer the feeling that your presentation is going to be an event that will last forever in people's minds.

◆ *Proposal:* With a strong proposal step, you will keep your customers on the edge of their seats. First, restate the customer's needs—as you have determined them through discovery—and check in with those present to verify that your understanding is complete and accurate. Check to see if there are other needs. Once this is done, state your purpose for the presentation and make a strong benefit statement, such as:

"Mary, during our previous meetings, you voiced some major concerns about your present situation. During those meetings, you indicated that there was a gap between the results you're currently realizing and your hope for improvement in the future. I am really excited today because my purpose is to present you with some unique new ideas that will close the gap and result in more productivity and profitability."

◆ *Solution:* In this step, you make your selling statements. You tell the customer what your resolution is—its features, then the advantages—and how your solution will work. Finally, you tell your customer the benefits.

The benefit statement is the most important thing you can say about your solution. It's the benefit that highlights the value of your proposed solution. Always link your solution to the customer's needs. If your benefit statements do not address those needs—and help close the gap between what the customer *wants* and what the customer is currently getting—then you will get a less than enthusiastic reaction.

Regrettably, some customers know the price of everything and the value of nothing. Make your benefit statements so impactful that they take the customer's focus off the price and refocus him on the value of your solution.

If you don't back up your selling statements with proof, you are asking the customer to make a major leap of faith. Prove the value of your solution by backing up your selling statements with the use of appropriate evidence—testimonials, demonstrations, exhibits, graphs, and statistics. These selling supports will help back up your claims by adding credibility to your solution.

Establish important differences between you and your competitor. When you are selling your ideas, you are in an evaluative atmosphere. People are going to be judging the merits and the price of your proposed solution against those of your competitor. Work hard to create a dramatic contrast between your benefits and your competitor's. Remember, though, the bottom line is value. Do you add more value? All things being equal, *you* make the difference, and your passion can be an exciting dimension that separates you from your rival.

✦ *Summary:* This is the step that brings your presentation into focus. It is in the summary step that you review the customer's problem, restate the solution, and summarize the benefits. For example:

"Mary, it's clear that a problem exists that must be resolved. As I pointed out, our solution will address this problem in a positive manner, and as a result, you will experience the following benefits— increased efficiency, more productivity, and increased profits."

Throughout your presentation, use response checks. These are a critical component of your presentation, because each response check takes the customer's temperature and tests the impact of your presentation on the customer. Consider suspending the presentation at appropriate times and response-checking as follows:

"In what ways does the solution I proposed address the problem?"

"Mary, what are some of your feelings, based on what I have just presented you?"

"What do you think about the proposed solution?"

Any good sales presentation is adjusted and modified to align itself with any new needs the customer might bring up. Another positive to the response check is that it gets the customer involved and makes him a partner in creating the solution.

After you do an attitude check, listen to the angel on your shoulder—the inner voice that's guiding you to do the right thing.

✔ **Be poised and diplomatic.**

Avoid confrontations and debates during the sales presentation. Prepare yourself to handle aggressive reactions. For instance, if your customer is protective of what he has been able to accomplish before you showed up on the scene, don't attack his current approach to the situation directly—even though you'd like to point out its deficiency or suggest a better way. Instead, acknowledge the customer's success in the past and, by asking the customer, explore how he was able to achieve such a level of excellence. Then diplomatically demonstrate how, with his guidance and support, your ideas will add a degree of excellence to the customer's current level of success using your rival's products and services.

When you encounter a customer's objection, use LAER:

✦ *Listen* to the customer's concern, and try to understand the customer's point of view.

✦ *Acknowledge* the customer's objections or questions with a concerned facial expression or a supportive comment such as, "I see what you mean. That's a good question to which I will try to respond in a helpful way." Acknowledging lets the customer know that you're trying to be helpful and creates a positive platform for your next step.

✦ *Explore*. Here, you attempt to deepen your understanding of the customer's objections, doubts, or bothersome questions. Here you reiterate and clarify:

"In other words, Mary, if I understand your question, you are concerned about our ability to perform as it relates to timing. Is my understanding of your questions accurate and complete?"

A well-executed exploratory step helps you identify the key issues you have to deal with and paves the way to the response step.

✦ *Respond*. In this step you are providing a suitable answer to the customer's objection or critical question. Your response could end up sounding something like this:

"Mary, now that I understand the concern you have, let me respond to it by saying . . ."

LAER—listening, acknowledging, exploring, and responding—is a contingency strategy that you use to address the customer during the sales transaction. LAER helps you deal with customer-centered issues throughout your presentation. LAER is a great way to say you care.

Closure is the natural thing to do when you have completed your presentation. But before you turn your mind to closing, you need to do everything in your power to make your presentation a stellar event.

✔ **Practice, practice, practice.**
If you don't make sales presentations on a regular basis, you get stale and undisciplined. Remember, selling is a skill-based profession, and if you want to maintain a competitive advantage, your performance will have to surpass your opponent's.

Before you "go on" in front of the customer, practice your presentation at least several times. Practice will help you get focused and mentally prepared. It will help you win the business!

✔ **Tap into your spiritual resources.**

Believe it or not, I never go on a sales call without saying a prayer. This may not be your cup of tea. Nevertheless, prayer helps me tap into my spiritual resources and it provides me with the confidence and energy to excel. Oh, yes—I make sales calls to global organizations that are so formal, stiff, and corporate, you can hear arteries hardening when you enter the room. And believe it or not, before the presentation I sing three songs with my presentation team: "Row, Row, Row Your Boat," "Three Blind Mice," and the first verse of the Marine Corps hymn.

I know this sounds nuts, but it absolutely works. Singing three songs and saying a prayer helps you blow off some excessive nervousness, puts a smile on your face, and programs your attitude and spirit to be positive and animated.

◆　◆　◆

When he had finished the points of The Way, the Mentor paused, reflecting for a moment.

"We have talked about making the presentation using positive contact, proposal, solution, and summary. We have talked about using response checks to locate the customer's mind-set, and we have talked about using LAER to clear objections during your sales presentation.

"I feel like we still have to talk about one of the most important actions in the entire presentation," he continued, looking from Tim to Jill. "I think you can understand why your sales presentations need to be spotlight events. Your selling statements must be passionate—and that means you have to convince yourself before you can expect to persuade others. But there's something else—"

The Mentor paused. "You have to be totally prepared to move to the final step. You must be ready to ask for the business—that is, for the customer's agreement to move forward on your recommendations. It's called closing."

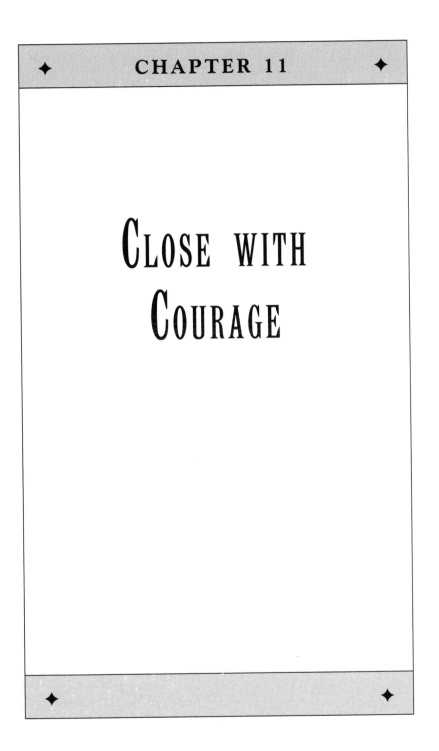

# CHAPTER 11

# CLOSE WITH COURAGE

# The Key to Closing

*Closing is a strategic moment that represents a test of courage and inner strength. Failing to close is not completing your mission.*

"**D**id you ever meet someone who makes brilliant sales presentations—but they're a bust when it comes to closing?" asked Tim.

"That sounds like a leading question," said the Mentor.

"Well, it's not *me* I'm talking about," Tim protested.

"Oh, no, of course not," Jill interjected. "Tim was just asking—kind of . . . theoretically." She waved her hand.

"That's right. Theoretically."

"Now, hold on a minute." The Mentor laughed. "If you're just a little bit—well—hesitant when it comes to closing, I can't exactly fault you." He sighed. "I was once a master of the a-hem, a-hem close. I was so fearful of closing, I used to engage in thirty minutes of throat clearing. I swear, I completely lost control of my senses. I was so consumed by anxiety, I would show up with my stomach in knots. I believe my jitter factor measured 9.9 on the Richter scale."

Tim was openmouthed.

"What's the matter?" asked the Mentor, noting his expression. "You don't believe it."

"I *do* believe it," Tim replied. "That's what's so incredible. If it could happen to you, it could happen to anyone."

"It's a feeling of impending doom, hanging over you like an executioner's ax, when you know you have to go in and close," Jill noted. "I can't imagine anything worse. I feel like I'm going to get my head lopped off if I ask for the order."

The Mentor grimaced as he was struck by a memory. "Do you know, my hands used to actually shake? For me, closing was like looking down the barrel of the customer's gun. I wish I could say I became brave under adversity." He winced.

"I'm afraid I was often guilty of failure to fire. I sat in solemn silence, like a spectator waiting for the climactic scene. When I tried to close, my voice was controlled, but beneath the surface there was an edge of desperation. I was demoralized and dispirited. Every close was a gut-wrenching experience—and every no was a personal rejection. Even though I knew a lot of the pressure was self-inflicted, I still had a paralyzing fear of failing. I was so frightened I thought I'd freeze completely. And because I couldn't close, I had an even tougher time trying to ask strong discovery questions, raise a price, or handle a simple customer objection. Sometimes I was gripped by an overwhelming feeling of helplessness. I was just insufficiently bold in confronting the situation. And then, after not asking for the order, I would feel guilt and self-pity. At the outset of my business career, I would also avoid confrontation at all costs, and I would buckle and sheepishly give in on minor issues. I wouldn't fight for anything—least of all, an order."

"It's hard to believe you went through all that," said Jill. "You seem to know exactly what to do, and when to do it."

"I was selling for years before I realized that you didn't automatically get an order after a strong presentation," the Mentor recalled. "I learned that I had to *ask* for an order—to really look the customer in the eye and *ask*. And that meant I needed the skills for this purpose. Make no mistake about it," he added. "Closing is a test of courage. In some cases, you're looking into the face of the dragon."

"The *fear*—where does that come from?" Tim wanted to know.

"I think it's quite natural," the Mentor replied. "When salespeople don't try to close, they're simply afraid of failing and being embarrassed, worried that their fragile sense of personal worth can't stand up under the shattering blow of a turndown. I know from experience it's hard to close if you are plagued with guilt, low self-esteem, and lack of confidence. Selling is a profession where courage is rewarded. Low self-esteem is a trap that paralyzes you. And some salespeople sound like they're resigned to a sad ending. You can hear it in their voices and see it in their faces.

"People with little confidence will shy away from closing because they will not run the risk of putting their fragile self-esteem on the line. And they take 'No' personally, as a denial of their worth. They read disrespect into the customer's refusal to purchase.

"The only way to find out is to take a responsible risk—

and ask for the order. It takes leadership to close with confidence in your cause. As one friend said, 'No request, no possibility.' "

"Well, maybe some people just can't do it," observed Jill.

The Mentor nodded. "You know, when I became a manager, I used to think that some people weren't cut out to close—that closing was just not their way. Their lips couldn't shape the words and their hearts couldn't do the deed. I felt so strongly about this that I would not send shaky salespeople out to wrap up a deal if I knew they couldn't ask for an order. I felt it was bad for everyone. So I would team them up with field-tested veterans who could pull the trigger—or I would go along with them and do it myself. I would feel good, and the poor salesperson would feel empty. Because salespeople who don't close die a little every day."

The Mentor paused thoughtfully. "But I was wrong about this, and I have long since changed my mind. If you can ask someone out on a date—or if you've had the courage to ask someone to marry you—you know you can run the risk of rejection. And that means you can close. You just have to want something badly enough. And you have to convince yourself you can do it. It's an emotional decision. It takes bravery."

"Are you going to give us a magic close?" Tim inquired. "It seems like every successful salesperson has some favorite close that works best for them."

"I could teach you many ways to close," said the Mentor, "but none of them will work unless you have the courage to use them. When it comes to asking for the business, one ounce of guts is worth a ton of talent."

"I think you're leaving something out," Tim interjected.

"What's that?"

"Well, what about the customer who just puts you on hold—the customer who always says, 'Your proposal is interesting. I'll get back to you'?"

"That's the worst!" Jill agreed. "That's the kiss of death."

"I don't know what it is," Tim observed, "but some customers seem to always want to delay a decision to buy until the last minute. They seem to want to be sure they are making the best decision and that everyone is behind them. In other words, they may be hovering somewhere between wanting you to exceed their wildest dreams while at the same time they're engaged by their most awful fear—that you won't perform."

"Well, there's one certain way to set their fears at rest," observed the Mentor.

"What's that?" asked Jill.

"Just say, '*Try me!*'" the Mentor replied. "Believe it or not, that close can set you apart." He smiled at the recollection of a recent incident. "I was in the grocery store the other day, looking for hot sauce—among other things. When I located the seasonings section, I was bombarded by dozens of different choices. But only one struck my fancy. It was Yucatan Sunshine Habanero Pepper Sauce. At the top of the bottle was a label, with words that shouted out for attention: 'Try me!' I jumped for joy when I spotted this request for action. And I reached out and snatched up a bottle of the hot sauce, even though it was more expensive than the others on the shelf. The lesson here is, if you want to stand out from the crowd, be the only one who says, '*Try me, I'll do a brilliant job for you.*'"

"And you *have* to make that promise if a customer is leaving behind another supplier," observed Tim. "*Try me!* is almost a challenge."

"It is—in the thoughtful sense of the word," the Mentor replied. Pausing for a moment, he added, "Some customers find it easier to change religions than to change suppliers. For them, switching over to your program is a very big deal."

"But you *can* get them to do it," said Tim. "It's just a matter of knowing how. Can you suggest a way?"

The Mentor smiled before nodding. "Let me try." He looked from Tim to Jill, then back again. "What I'm about to tell you is inspired by actual events that happened to me."

## ✦✦✦ THE WAY ✦✦✦

✔ **Be difficult to say no to.**

Never let fatigue and the odds discourage you from being persistent. Cause people to take you seriously. The longer the customer lives without your solution, the less he thinks he needs it. And the longer the decision is delayed, the less your chances of being successful. Pursue a commitment with dogged determination. Remember, you haven't closed until you ask for a concrete commitment and get one. Keep in mind that customers give business to those they find it the most difficult to say no to. *Be* difficult to say no to.

✔ **Give the customer options.**

It's always easier to close on options because you avoid boxing the customer in. Options give the customer the power of choice. By asking the customer to make a choice, you avoid an all-or-nothing situation. A choice on a minor point takes the pressure off Yes or No and converts the close into an either/or.

For example, "Tom, we have essentially two implementation options: We can begin immediately or we can start implementation the early part of next month. Which option appears to be the soundest alternative for you?"

✔ **Keep your eye on the prize.**

Stay focused. Don't let your fears be the focus of your attention—it's the opportunities you envision with this particular customer that you should be thinking about. Remember, not closing will cost you dearly. It will probably cost you the business.

✔ **Never waver.**

See closing as the action step that unleashes the power of you and your organization to benefit your customer. A don't-ask-for-it attitude is deadly in selling. And not closing is a serious failure that shuts down the possibility of moving ahead. View closing as your obligation or individual responsibility and a courageous move that makes everything possible for the customer.

✔ **Pull the trigger.**

Don't point the gun if you're not going to pull the trigger. In other words, don't put your heart and soul into developing and presenting a sales proposal if you're not going to ask for the order. The big-game salesperson knows when to pull the trigger and close. So will you.

✔ **Create a sense of urgency.**

Attach a time line to your close—today, now, Friday morning. A time line adds teeth to your close. For example, "When can I begin helping you increase productivity and profitability?" Or: "May I begin to support you in your efforts to reduce costs and increase efficiency today?"

✔ **Cross the finish line.**

Not closing is like dropping out of the race because you are fearful of losing. Remember that courage is fear that has said its prayers, and the value of this great struggle will fortify your resolve to complete the mission. Nothing is more important than the courage you bring to your sales responsibilities.

✔ **Get as high as a kite.**

Remember that the higher up in the organization you go, the easier it is to close at your asking price. Always, *always* seek out the highest authority, the king- and queen-makers. Sell them on your solution and on your commitment to resolve their needs. Don't be timid about this. Always ask your key contact for the opportunity to access top people. For example: "Besides you, Sarah, what other people in your organization should I be presenting this proposal to? Who else, like you, is vitally concerned about results? Will you guide me in contacting this person?"

✔ **Create an active memory.**

If you have a long selling cycle—and the decision will be made at a later date—take advantage of the delay. Facts become diluted, garbled, and muddled over a period of time, but your human qualities take over. The prevailing impression of *you* becomes the focal point. Create an active memory through follow-up calls, e-mails, faxed messages, letters— anything that will keep you active in your customer's mind. When it is certain that you won't get a decision on the spot, always use the next-step close: "Pat, inasmuch as we can't reach a decision today, can we at least decide on our next step—and would you give me some guidance as to what the next step should be?" Remember what I said earlier—no request, no possibilities.

✔ **Avoid postcall letdown.**

The excitement and exhilaration of getting the order can be all too fleeting. Relish your victory. Experience the joy within! Through fearless determination, you have paid the price to be a winner— and now you have the win that you deserve!

✦  ✦  ✦

"And—if you *don't* get the order?" asked Tim.

The Mentor smiled. "It wouldn't be the first time, would it?"

Jill laughed. "I think I've heard every objection that customers can think of. But I'm still stunned when they don't accept my solution."

"And everyone says that the sale begins when the customer says no." Tim chuckled. "Not for me."

"Just remember, the relationship isn't over," the Mentor said. "I know—the sudden letdown could leave you confused, frightened, anxious, low, and bewildered. It's a dispiriting loss."

Tim shook his head. "Sometimes you just can't get around that postcall letdown. You *know* it's over. You can feel it in your gut."

"You've never really lost the sale," said the Mentor. "Even when you're told, 'Your competitor got the business,' it's not the final word. I know of countless times when a salesperson, having been told no, hung tough and continued to actively call on the customer. He was just alert and aware—and he waited for the competitor to stub his toe. It could happen the very first time your customer tries your competitor's solution. Believe me, it will be the salesperson watching and working in the wings—the person who demonstrates a constant vigilance—who will be tapped to come in and rescue the situation."

"I know a lot of salespeople who back away if they can't close," said Jill. "They figure that since they've given their sales presentation their best shot, there's nothing more they can do."

"That's pretty shortsighted," said Tim. "The environment is changing so fast, I figure if I'm standing by when my competitor drops the ball, I'll be the first to pick it up again."

"You'll need to do more than stand by and wait in the wings," cautioned the Mentor. "There's another quality that's essential."

"What's that?" asked Jill.

The Mentor smiled. "In your grandmother's day, it would have been called good old-fashioned perseverance. I call it persistence."

# CHAPTER 12

# PERSIST WITH DETERMINATION

# The Key to Persistence

*It's not the competitor who decides whether you have won or lost. The only time you fail to make the sale is when you decide to stop the process.*

At the word "persistence," Tim was jolted by a memory. "I remember when I was being interviewed for this job," he recalled. "The interviewer told me that persistence would take me to the top."

Jill laughed.

"What's so funny?"

"Well, of course he said the same thing to me," Jill replied. "He told me, 'I'll take the person with staying power— any day—over a flash-and-dash sprinter that never makes the finish line.' "

"Oh, yeah," Tim agreed. "I'd forgotten that one. He must use that line on everyone he interviews for a sales position."

"So—what's it mean?" The Mentor seemed to be waiting for both of them to answer.

"Persistence?" Tim asked. At the Mentor's nod, he replied, "It means knocking on doors. Never giving up. Always getting back to the customer."

"Anything else?"

"Putting your best foot forward," Jill added. "Never acting blasé when you're dealing with customers."

"Yes." The Mentor regarded them as if waiting for more.

"I give up." Jill was perplexed. "What are we missing?"

"What about the internal part of it?" the Mentor asked. "What *creates* persistence?"

Tim was puzzled by the Mentor's question. "Well—you've got to have a gung-ho attitude. I figure persistent salespeople are the ones who get up in the morning and ask, 'Am I gaining ground or losing ground?' And if they're losing ground, they want to do something about it."

Jill had been watching the Mentor's expression while Tim replied. Now she put in: "But you're talking about something else, aren't you?"

The Mentor nodded. "I'm talking about *appetite*," he said. "Great salespeople bring a ravenous appetite for victory to their selling activities. In the final analysis, how badly you really want the business will determine your degree of perseverance.

"To be persistent, you need to acquire a taste for victory and achievement," he went on. "You need an all-consuming desire to reach your goal. Persistence puts you in command of your work—and gives you immense power.

"Only you decide whether you have won or lost—no one else. You are never really out of it until you decide you are. You're always faced with competition, and that means you're in a constant struggle for supremacy. Persistence should become a conditioned reflex: As soon as the gun goes off, you automatically go into action."

"But what about the salesperson who says she doesn't

really care about winning every time out?" asked Jill. "What if she says she'll get her share of the business sooner or later? She can still be persistent—can't she?"

"Absolutely not," replied the Mentor. "That's what is called a consolation mentality—settling for runner-up status. I've never seen a person with a consolation mentality become a consistent winner. It takes dash and vigor to be persistent. If you don't have a taste for winning, it's like playing the game of selling with an empty gun.

"Life experience has shown me that the salespeople who are most persistent clearly outperform their competitors," the Mentor continued thoughtfully. "That's what gives them a sense of purpose. Regrettably, for some salespeople, 'You made a fine presentation' is all they need to feel fulfilled."

The Mentor shook his head. "In selling, you don't get the Spirit of the Game Award for trying. It's only victory that brings joy. When it comes to persistence, the prize isn't always won by the fastest—but goes to the person who keeps on running. If you're not persistent in selling, you'll come dangerously close to failing."

"And how do you know when you're *too* persistent?" Tim wanted to know. "Surely there's the point where you cross the line."

"If I push *too* hard and appear to be using arm-twisting tactics, the customer is going to get fed up," Jill agreed.

The Mentor shook his head. "I don't agree," he replied. "Some people look at persistence as being awkward and embarrassing and personally distasteful. But persistence should be an exciting time, because it keeps your opportunities from drifting away. It's what I call tense time. Don't be guilty of wilting away in the heat of pursuit."

Tim remained skeptical. "But what about resistance from the customer? You mean that you'd *never* give up—even if the situation looks hopeless?"

The Mentor regarded Tim quizzically. "And what would you call 'hopeless'?"

"Well, for instance, when the customer says, 'We'll be in touch.' "

"Those awful words!" Jill laughed.

"Awful is right," the Mentor agreed. "But if they say they'll be in touch, it just means *you* be in touch. You can't stand pat, no matter what happens. That's just putting your head in the sand. Remember, the only time you fail to make the sale is when you decide to stop the process. But fear of failure is like electricity—it can kill you or it can motivate you. Use that fear to stimulate your competitive juices."

"But how do you know you're not just spinning your wheels?" asked Tim.

"Sometimes we're dealing with organizations that seem to take joy in putting salespeople on the rack or studying your recommendation to death," Jill observed.

The Mentor nodded understandingly. "It's easy to get discouraged by the environment you have to deal with," he observed. "You can't let yourself be overwhelmed. Even though you may be working in some environments that seem like toxic landfills when it comes to being fair and responsible, stick to your guns. Don't be deterred from making a fierce and enduring effort to succeed even though the customer treats you poorly or puts you on hold.

"Troublesome customers are staples in a salesperson's daily diet. But you have to be smart as well as tenacious and aggressive. Remember, someone is selling them something. And by all rights, that someone should be you."

"But aren't there customers who actually prefer a less aggressive, laid-back style of staying in touch?" Jill ventured.

"Maybe," the Mentor replied. "But from most of the signs I'm seeing, the relaxed give-and-take of the past has given way to a sense of urgency that customers appreciate in salespeople.

"Remember, in this environment your goal with every customer is to achieve Preferred Position. That comes with a price tag—and the price tag is persistence.

"You may be in an unresponsive environment, but you need to be persistent even when people are elusive, remote, unapproachable, and standoffish. Persistence takes a bottomless inner strength. You have to want to be more successful than your competitor. It's what you need in order to achieve a supreme advantage in a customer relationship. You always need to feel the excitement for selling."

"Just one person saying no can turn the decision against you," Tim agreed.

"If you run up against one person who's against your proposal, you have a hurdle," the Mentor observed. "If you run up against two or more, you have a wall."

"Well, how do you get *everyone* on your side of the wall?" Jill asked.

"People tend to endorse, support, and activate what they help create," the Mentor observed. "Let everyone have their fingerprints on your sales proposal. When you're persisting, you want to get everyone on board carrying your banner."

"But *how?*" demanded Tim.

The Mentor considered a moment. When he next spoke, it was to outline The Way.

# ✦✦✦ THE WAY ✦✦✦

✔ **Be there, be there, be there.**

Frequent contact is one of the strongest forms of bonding. It creates an obligation to take you seriously. Let your competitor be the one to rest, take recess, and catch his breath. When salespeople fail, it's from a lack of urgency and intensity. Don't be a quitter. Don't let the tense time of pursuit weaken you.

✔ **Smother your customer with attention.**

Show your stick-to-itiveness. Refuse to let anyone put the kibosh on you. Be a constant presence. Your customers will soon get the idea that you are not to be put off or discouraged easily. Not all customers will look at you with a kind eye, but the more often you show up, the better your chances.

✔ **Find ways to stay in front of the customer.**

There are some customers you have to approach on bended knee. Shoot out a revision to your proposal. Cut out an article and send your customer a copy. Send your customers postcards, flowers, pictures—or anything else that will keep you within their line of sight. Leave a positive emotional memory in your customer's soul. You want your presence felt in your absence.

✔ **Err on the side of doing too much.**

In a sense, persistence takes doggedness—and a self-reliant, can-do spirit. Keep yourself on the customer's agenda. Even when the customer sets up a wall of separation, focus your passion on undistracted action. Be guilty of boldness instead of hesitation. Make the telephone call you have been avoiding. Persistent people view what they're doing as the means to a hope-filled future.

✔ **Avoid self-limiting behavior.**

Some salespeople believe they are too busy to write a follow-up note, to send a fax, or to call for an e-mail update on where things stand. Others say they won't do this for fear they will be considered pushy and a pest. Baloney! Go for it. You're nuts if you don't press on!

✔ **Take risks.**

At times, you have to be very brave as a salesperson. Emotionally soft people are not very persistent. You need passion and chutzpah. Remember, when you do take a risk, rarely will the customer fault you for trying. Those that *lay off* get *put off* and *left out*.

✔ **Get to the corner office.**

You have to get beyond being in the customer's Rolodex and get onto his order pad. Spirited determination will propel you to a stepped-up perseverance posture. Whenever you're making a proposal, use the opportunity to extend your influence. For instance, "In addition to you, Elizabeth, who else should I be meeting with in order to demonstrate the benefits of my value proposition?" Don't squander the opportunity to make contacts. Meet as many people as possible in your customer's business, and convert them to advocates.

✔ **Stay in hot pursuit.**

Your last up-front and close, person-to-person sales call need not be your last personal contact with the customer. Most of the time, the decision is made in your absence. But you can't maintain a passive stance while the decision-making is in progress— that could give your competitor an advantage if he is a hard worker. If he bears down and initiates a lot of follow-up activity, you could be left in the dust. He could, as a result, impress the customer with his determination and thus tilt the odds in his favor.

✔ **Get to the canary who sings.**

Always make an effort to get to the highest levels in your customer's organization. Sustain your undaunted efforts. Get by the ceremonial figureheads, gatekeepers, naysayers, and the VPs in

Charge of Rare Events to put yourself squarely in front of the highest authority. The canary who sings is the guy or gal whose nod of the head signals victory or defeat. They're the ones who can write an order. You've got to get to the top people and create an advocacy. To do this, you have to maneuver your way through the corridors of power and finally get a chance to dance with the giants.

✔ **Lift your chin up.**

Credit yourself with being ambitious, dependable, and an inspired professional. Persistence takes a positive and assured person. You need to be diligent and determined, with unrelenting staying power. Always do *more* rather than *less*.

✔ **Prevent the momentum shift.**

Never let the momentum swing in favor of your competitor. The fact is, the customer will cool off on your sales proposal unless you camp out on his doorstep. Getting the order can be a time-consuming and exhausting contest. This kind of situation favors the persistent person—but you have to be vigilant. When dealing with customer groups, it could take a long time before a decision is made. And the longer the decision is delayed, the less your chances of being successful. So always maintain a frequent presence.

✔ **Get back in the hunt.**

Always be looking for new opportunities. Ask yourself the question, "Do I win and quit, or do I win and *never* quit?" After the hunt, the catch, and the victory, some salespeople take a breather vacation. This is nuts! Use the positive energy from your recent win to propel you into your next great sales challenge. Skip the vacation!

✦  ✦  ✦

"If you're not persistent, if you lack a sense of urgency, you could languish in uncertainty," the Mentor concluded. "Imagine not knowing whether or not you could have been successful."

In the moment's silence that followed, Jill found her mind coming alive with new ideas. Only a short time before, she had been struggling to think of new ways to create a sense of urgency with her customers.

"Even when you think you got the sale, it seems like you always have to deal with the customer's late-hour 'Oh-by-the ways.' " Jill shook her head as she recalled some of these phrases. " 'Oh, by the way, we want you to throw in *this* or *that* as part of the deal.' When these kinds of requests for concessions appear late in the sales transaction, they can turn into deal-breakers."

"Yes, they can—but they don't have to," agreed the Mentor. "When you hear those requests, you know it's time to negotiate. You need to put your intellect and courage into action—and negotiate a fair deal for everyone. Now is a good time to ask for divine guidance."

# CHAPTER 13

# NEGOTIATE FROM STRENGTH

# The Key to Successful Negotiations

*In negotiations there can be no losers. The outcome has to be a win for all concerned. And fairness is the glue that keeps the process together—which means shared risk, shared commitment, and shared prosperity.*

"What's so difficult about negotiating?" Tim wondered aloud. "Most of the time, there's no problem."

The Mentor winced.

"What's the matter?" Jill asked, noting his expression.

"It's that phrase—'No problem'," explained the Mentor.

"What's wrong with it?" asked Tim. "Why should 'No problem' be a problem?"

"Well, I'll tell you what happened," the Mentor went on. "I remember a good friend telling me that his salespeople suffered from the No Problem Syndrome. It goes like this: The customer says, 'I want . . .' and the salesperson says, 'No problem!' The customer says, 'We need . . .' and the salesperson says, 'No problem!' The customer says, 'You must . . .' and the salesperson says, 'No problem!' "

"So—it sounds like they were in perfect agreement," noted Tim.

The Mentor shook his head. "Maybe, but as my friend said, 'The trouble is, *No problem* equals *No profit!*'"

"I see what you mean." Tim laughed.

"And that's why you need to be able to negotiate," the Mentor continued. "Negotiating is not a game. It's not a matter of knocking off a sale, beating out your competitor, or winning a bidding war. Nor is it making a lot of concessions.

"Negotiating is a fair exchange. It's a goodwill gesture that moves you toward a win/win solution. And the outcome of negotiating is that you build *anam cara* and improve your position.

"I believe that two parties can always negotiate as long as they both recognize fairness. This is the glue that keeps the negotiation process together. Absence of fairness creates distrust, resentment, and bitterness. Without fairness, there will be distance between you and your customer. Any negotiation will ultimately be sabotaged. Absence of fairness creates negative tension in the negotiation and ultimately causes the breakdown of the transaction.

"In many of today's negotiations, the customer is looking for concessions," the Mentor continued. "There are terms and conditions of sale that they want free of charge—such as lower price and better credit terms. Or they make unusual and expensive requests. If you give in to their requests, the profitability of the sale goes south.

"In reality, giving in to profit-draining concessions is the same as yielding or giving up. If you knuckle under to the customer's demands in order to win the business, an imbalance occurs that makes the negotiations lopsided."

"But we all make concessions *sometimes*," Jill observed.

"Indeed," Tim agreed. "You know, what we're talking

about right now is grimly reminiscent of the times when customers asked me for deep discounts—or they held me up for cruel and unusual terms and conditions of sale."

"Concessions are in large measure by-products of an unconvinced customer," replied the Mentor. "The customer's need for a concession becomes more important when you've not done a good job of selling yourself and your benefits. So getting the customer excited about your solution reduces the pressure to make concessions.

"Instead of making concessions, you need to *influence* the customer to take action—while at the same time reducing the customer's need for profit-draining concessions. Being influential means that you get someone to act on your point of view or your belief—transferring your positive energy to another person in order to produce a tangible result.

"Being influential also means that you are a person of action—and you are going to throw all your assets into performing for the customer."

"You know what?" Jill interjected. "I think the biggest negotiations challenge I face every day is trying to sell my proposed solution to the customer at what I believe to be a fair and equitable price. It seems as though every time I submit my pricing, the customer objects and engages me in a bone-crushing round of negotiations. And some negotiations wind up becoming a bruising contest of extended haggling and squabbling over price."

"Same here," Tim agreed. "Sometimes the negotiations become so ballistic that I feel shell-shocked. We reach an impasse, and the transaction breaks down, with me folding under pressure and reducing the price. Clearly, the customers

I call on are constantly looking for a bargain-basement deal on everything."

"And if you cut the price," said Jill, "it's like saying you charged the customer too much to begin with."

"Cutting the price flies in the face of everything a professional salesperson stands for," agreed the Mentor. "It's a very forbidding state of affairs."

"But if I don't cut the price, my competitor will," Tim complained.

"We still have a responsibility to ourselves and our organization," the Mentor said, a note of grimness in his voice. "We live in a brutal, no-frills pricing arena. Customers are being forced to insist on the best possible prices. It's part of their job. For some, however, it's just part of their nature to hassle you for a pricing concession. It's part of the game.

"And some customers are not going to praise you for doing a good job, for fear that they'll hand you the paddle to whack them with the next time pricing comes up. So you have to learn to live without a lavish amount of praise."

"Some customers are so price-sensitive, they throw a nickel around like it was a manhole cover." Tim laughed.

"But if we are not careful, we could become the witless victims, giving in to price concessions instead of sticking up for our prices," said the Mentor. "When you stick up for your pricing, you are sticking up for yourself." He shook his head. "The fact is, some salespeople take the low road or easy way out. They don't stick up for their prices because they are insecure and suffer from low self-esteem. They 'give the stuff away' because they are intimidated by the customer and because they are starved for the customer's approval. They are more concerned about the customer liking them and keeping the peace than they are about selling their product and service at a fair price. You will often hear them say, 'I didn't want to lose the business.'

"Some of these salespeople act like double agents and misplace their loyalty," the Mentor continued. "They buy into the customer's reason for needing a price reduction, and they put all of their energy into convincing their organizations of the legitimacy of a price concession. So, remember, price becomes important to the extent that you and your benefits are not. If you present a formidable presence, you will be less likely to be hit on for pricing concessions."

The Mentor's face flushed when he shared his next thought. "Personally, I have a difficult time with a salesperson who thinks his prices are always too high, and who is constantly complaining about not getting the business because he is not price competitive. This kind of salesperson you wish on your competition.

"They are the kind of salespeople who will take business under undesirable conditions and thereby discount the value of what they are selling. Deep down inside, I like pricing-aggressive salespeople. It's a sign of backbone and grit. It's also an indicator of their confidence in their ability to perform."

The Mentor reflected for a moment—and when he spoke again, his voice was insistent. "Don't give anything away free! Always get something back! As a rule, people in business do not value and appreciate what they get for nothing.

"My friend Rabbi Daniel Lapin confirmed this notion when he recently told me, 'He who does something for another is bound to the recipient by far stronger emotional ties than the recipient is to the giver.' This explains why, counterintuitively, parents will always love children unconditionally, since parents are the givers. Children, however, as the constant receivers or recipients of good, are—sadly—often known to be a little less loving.

"This principle applies to the whole idea of negotiations," the Mentor went on. "The party who does the greatest amount of giving in the negotiation process is clearly the one who is making more of a commitment to the relationship. This situation sets up an imbalance in the relationship, and eventually the giver harbors feelings of unfairness.

"Now, if you as a sales professional feel as though you got a raw deal, you probably won't appreciate, celebrate, or care enough about it. This is not good. You'll probably find an unconscious way of paying the customer back for not treating you fairly. It's a very dangerous state of affairs."

"But you're talking as if we call the shots," observed Tim. "There's always the implied threat that our customers will go with our competitors. What can you say when the customer demands a lower price?"

"You want my recommendation? Well, here it is. I'd always ask the two most important questions when you're confronted with a price concession request," replied the Mentor. "If you're asked to lower your prices, for example, always acknowledge the request and then follow up by asking, 'What are you trying to accomplish by asking me for a lower price?'

"The typical response will be something like, 'I am trying to keep my costs down.'

"As you can see, the customer is asking for the end and

not the means—the means being the lower price and the end being keeping his costs down.

"It is then appropriate to ask the second question: 'Would you be open to an alternative to me cutting the price if this alternative would help you achieve the same result—keeping your costs down?'

"Now you have to provide your rationale by laying out a cost-benefit analysis, demonstrating that the benefits of your proposed solution will more than offset the additional costs involved.

"Do you see what I'm getting at?" the Mentor asked, looking from Tim to Jill. "We're talking about the idea of converting profit-draining concessions into profit-producing exchanges.

"The way I see it, negotiation is a bilateral agreement, or trading one thing for another," the Mentor continued. "And that's also the definition of an exchange—it's doing just that. It's saying to the customer, 'I will give you this in return for that'—a reciprocal agreement that is often referred to in the Latin as *quid pro quo*.

"And comfort in negotiating a fair exchange takes training—preparation and skill, discipline and courage. In fact, the preparation for negotiating is sometimes more important than the execution."

"Preparation—" Jill mused. "Now there's an interesting topic. I do it all in my head and hope for the best."

"Me, too," Tim agreed. "I wish there was another way to prepare. I'd feel a lot more confident of success."

"Well, there is a way," the Mentor replied. "But you have to anticipate the customer's demands—and then prepare a list of what you will need from the customer in return."

"What do you mean?" asked Jill.

"Anticipating the customer's demand means you make an educated guess about what the customer wants as part of the deal. For instance, you might anticipate that as a condition of sale the customer will ask for a lower price, better payment terms, and a well-documented assurance of quality. Write these down on one side of a piece of paper.

"Then prepare the exchange—that is, what the customer can offer in exchange if you can meet her demands. What the customer might give in exchange, for example, are future opportunities, referrals, or a long-term contract. Write these down on the other side of the paper."

"But that's all preparation," said Tim. "I might anticipate what I *think* the customer is going to demand, and I know how to prepare my response. But what happens during the actual exchange?"

"Remember that Latin term I used—*quid pro quo?*" the Mentor asked. "It's critical to the exchange."

"But how?" Tim asked. "What actually *happens* when you activate the negotiation?"

"Well, it's simply a matter of turning to the customer and asking, 'If I can give you *this*, would you meet me part of the way . . . and provide me with *that?*'

"Or you could suggest, 'I'll do my best to respond to your request. However, in order to provide you with _____, I'll need your support to make this possible. What I will ask for in exchange is the following. . . .'

"Once the exchange has been made," the Mentor went on, "always check for fairness by asking the customer, 'Does this sound fair to you?' "

"You make it sound so easy!" exclaimed Jill.

"Well, some negotiations are easier than others," the Mentor responded, "especially if you have *anam cara* and Preferred Position with the customer. But there are some principles that hold true for nearly *all* negotiations."

And then he told them The Way.

## ✦✦✦ THE WAY ✦✦✦

✔ **Head off surprises.**

While you are in Discovery and Resolution, try to flush out the "Oh-by-the-ways" that the customer could spring on you after you have submitted your sales proposal and pricing. Ask the question, "What other needs are likely to come up later that I should be aware of now?" Asking questions like this will bring into focus terms and conditions of sale that should be taken into consideration before you develop your pricing strategy.

✔ **Act as though you have a backlog of business.**

If you are shopping hungry—that is, you do not have a backlog of business and you're behind in your sales goals—you will negotiate from weakness. You may be inclined to make concessions that you otherwise wouldn't. So focus on the success you are currently having—and the success you *anticipate* having. This will give you the resolve to execute the exchange confidently.

✔ **Stand your ground.**

In negotiations, we cannot accede to every demand. Sometimes we are faced with some unpleasant choices. And that means you must have the guts to walk away from bad business. If you have exhausted all of your efforts—to no avail—it's better to "deselect" the customer who is totally unreasonable. That kind of customer is likely to drag you into unprofitable and dangerous waters. Bail out before this happens.

✔ **Resist temptation.**

Some customers will insist that you provide your solution at your competitor's price. But meeting your competitor's price is not worthy of you. After all, your presence in the customer relationship should be worth a higher price—and you're going to put more of yourself into the deal than your competitor would, and that is certainly worth something. Besides, if your competitor can sell it for less, then that's probably what it's worth.

✔ **Avoid ballpark estimates.**

Nine times out of ten, the ballpark estimates become binding when the customer wants to place his business. That also goes for quantity or large-volume purchases. Your highest-quantity price typically becomes the agreed-to price if you're not careful. Don't take the bait.

✔ **Don't get caught in the squeeze.**

Make sure you coach your boss into backing your terms-and-conditions-of-sale position. All too often, the customer will call your boss in an effort to get a better deal. If your boss caves in, it makes you look like an opportunistic schlepp without any power to cut the deal. And some managers are commonly referred to as "caves" because they drop the price at the blink of an eye.

As a salesperson, you should always play a full and constructive part in the negotiations. Tell your boss that you are under extreme pressure to lower the price, so he or she is not taken by surprise by a phone call from the customer. Brief your boss on the total pricing scenario so he has all the facts before he makes a decision. And ask him to put the customer on hold so that you are the one who goes back in with your pricing position.

✔ **Strike high.**

Negotiate at the highest level. And look expensive and upscale—so your customer sees you as a consummate professional and is not surprised by your price. If you negotiate with junior people, they may hammer away on price because they want to use a victory as a means to score points with their boss.

✔ **Everyone wins in negotiations.**

If you're thinking negative thoughts, then you'll tend to act out those negative thoughts in the form of nonproductive negotiation behavior—such as getting sore with the person—which may cause you to get flustered, disoriented, and unfocused. In some schools of thought, people regard negotiations as a confrontation vehicle where you are supposed to win as much as you can at a cost to the other person. This is wrong. Never think of your customer as your opponent. Think of your customer as a business partner.

*Confine the negotiations to the fewest people possible.* The larger the group you negotiate in, the more pressure you will get to give concessions. People will resist working with you for fear they'll come off looking too soft to the rest of the members of their negotiating team. Try to negotiate one-on-one with Mr. Big rather than doing this in a large assembly.

✔ **Sell your pricing.**

Always refer to your pricing as responsible, which means the price is fair for the value exchanged. All things being equal, you should be the one that makes the difference. Portray yourself as being worth the extra money.

✔ **Stay in the game.**

Even if you can't remotely match the competitor's price and you are passed over for the business, hang tough. It could be that the competitor's solution that's being sold for less proves inadequate. Or that he slips up the first time at bat. Always maintain a constant vigilance by keeping in frequent contact with the customer during your competitor's start-up or implementation phase.

✦  ✦  ✦

"But you can negotiate forever, if you're not careful," Tim observed.

"If you have a buy-off on the solution before you negotiate, then you and the customer both know you're moving toward the desired goal," the Mentor answered. "True, the negotiation may last a long time. In fact, you should always *ask* for separate time. This gives you the opportunity to slip out of the transaction and think things through. You'll be able to prepare a more thorough response."

"I always feel like my customers have more respect for me if I negotiate well," said Jill.

The Mentor nodded. "You're probably right. When you negotiate a fair deal that everyone feels is mutually beneficial, you demonstrate outstanding professionalism. By initiating and managing the negotiations—and being thoroughly prepared—you credential yourself and elevate your status. Professional negotiating promotes a sense of fairness, which is vital to building long-term relationships and deepening *anam cara*."

"But even so, you haven't really reached your destination until you get the deal and deliver the goods," said Jill.

"Yes, that's right," said the Mentor. "But along the way, you have to bounce back from setbacks. You must be able to climb the ladder from rejection to recovery."

# BOUNCE BACK FROM REJECTION

"The Ladder to Recovery? What's that?" Jill glanced at Tim. Was this something they were supposed to know already? But the shake of his head and his equally puzzled expression told her instantly—he didn't know either.

"Well, you know what I mean by *rejection*."

"Sure do!" Tim spelled out the letters in the air. First an "N." Then an "O."

Jill laughed. "That word gives me nightmares."

"But sometimes it's not spelled out so clearly," observed the Mentor.

"That's true," Jill agreed. "Sometimes it's the silent treatment."

"People who don't take your calls," put in Tim. "Or they don't acknowledge your messages."

"People can think up very creative ways to snub you," said Jill.

"Your business goes to the competition—"

"And then you're sacked"—Tim smiled wanly—"as the British would say."

The Mentor nodded. "Getting 'sent down' is what I've heard it called." He paused, studying his fingertips. "So . . . what happens to you internally when you feel the impact of rejection?" He looked up, his exploring gaze meeting Tim's and then Jill's. "How do you process it? How do you handle it? How do you deal with it?" he pursued.

"It's a problem, all right," agreed Jill. "You feel completely uninvolved and left out—but you still have to carry on business with other customers as usual. You have to deal with the customer who rejected you—at least at some level—and make absolutely certain your other customers don't suffer from the side effects of the pain you're in."

"I think I can help you there."

"How?" asked Tim.

"That's where the Ladder to Recovery comes in. It's a process for handling the negative effects of rejection. And at the same time, it allows you to keep working effectively with other customers."

"And it really helps?" asked Jill.

"It does—if you first understand what rejection is and how it affects us." The Mentor paused a moment, his expression solemn, before continuing. "Rejection leaves a bitter emotional residue. The more intense you feel about wanting the business, the more devastated you feel when you're let down. That's better than some salespeople who react to wins and losses with the same degree of blandness. But even so, don't be guilty of a miscalculated overreaction. You need a strategy for recovery that will position you for greater personal effectiveness—and lead to renewal."

"Okay, we're with you." Jill nodded. From Tim's expression she could tell he was just as eager to learn.

"Well, let's begin with that word you dread—the word 'No!' Why is it so awful to hear that word?" asked the Mentor.

"*Why?* Because it means I failed!" replied Jill. "I didn't get the business—and I blame myself. I lie awake at night wondering, 'What *didn't* I do right? What did I forget?'"

"Yeah," Tim agreed. "And if you let those thoughts get out of hand, it gets even worse than that. Like: 'Why doesn't this person like me? Why am I always being snubbed? I feel like the Heartbreak Kid.'"

"And what about the anger?" the Mentor put in.

Startled, Tim glanced at Jill. He could tell by her expression the Mentor had touched a raw nerve in her as well.

"We all contend with the anger," the Mentor continued, as if reading Tim's thoughts. "We're ambitious. We're competitive. We have high expectations and big dreams. When a customer gives you a big fat 'No,' all your lights go out. I used to sit there in stunned silence, a stony look of resignation on my face, emotionally disabled and bewildered, frozen into inaction. I was shattered, mystified, and confused—shaken to the core. But underneath it all was controlled anger."

"Did you ever blow up?" Tim asked sheepishly.

The Mentor responded with a pained smile. "You only have to do that once to realize what a mistake it is. Demonstrating anger is a luxury a salesperson cannot afford." He peered into Tim's eyes, an understanding look on his face. "Tim, we've all been guilty of an occasional miscalculated and harsh overreaction."

Tim could feel himself turning red.

"It's okay," the Mentor consoled him. "When you are rejected, it's a sickening experience. You feel devastated, shell-shocked. It saps your confidence. No *wonder* it rocks your world."

"How do you *deal* with it?" Jill was shaking her head. "I mean, I go numb. I limp out of the guy's office, and I'm so unsettled, I slink into the next sales call wearing a rejection grimace from ear to ear. After I've been rejected, I feel so uncomfortable about the relationship, I just want to disappear—I want to vanish off the face of the planet."

"I know," the Mentor said. "How well I know!" he added with a grim smile. "For me, rejection was a difficult moment. In my early days success was elusive because I couldn't handle rejection. It was like a bad hangover. The pain just kept hanging around.

"I would pay a heavy emotional price, because in rejecting my sales proposal, the customer was rejecting *me*. Deprived of the business, my confidence was shattered. I would lose heart, making a swift exit. It was as though the last nail was hammered into my coffin.

"The shame and embarrassment were so overwhelming that I would drag myself out of the customer's office hounded by self-pity and self-induced gloom. Rarely would I go back again, and thus I wrecked my chances for future business.

"Just remember, no matter what happens, the relationship isn't over." The Mentor studied Jill and Tim with a sympathetic and understanding gaze. "I know—the sudden fall from grace can leave you feeling low."

Jill nodded.

"But you can get over your loss," the Mentor continued. "To get over it, you have to work *through* it."

"Even if you've really lost the sale?" Tim looked skeptical. "I mean, sometimes you *know* it's over. You can feel it in your bones."

The Mentor shook his head. "You've never lost the sale—even when you've been told, 'Your competitor got the order.' Again, I know of countless times when a salesperson, having been told no, hung tough and continued to actively call on the customer. He remained alert and watched for the gal or guy who got the business to blow it the first time they were given the opportunity to solve the customer's problem. Believe me, it will be the salesperson in the wings, who has demonstrated a constant vigilance, who will be tapped to come in and rescue the situation."

Tilting back in his chair, the Mentor regarded Tim and Jill with unconcealed sympathy. Suddenly Tim was acutely aware of their vast difference in experience. How many times had he heard the word "no" in the few months of his fledgling career? The Mentor must have faced rejection hundreds of times—even thousands. What kind of vast endurance did it take to persevere in the face of such opposition?

"When you're rejected, all kinds of emotions boil up in you," the Mentor reflected with a faraway look. "You'd better be prepared to face frustration and stress. Many salespeople go into a state of denial, reliving the sales call and trying to change the ending. The nagging doubts and crushed hopes can sap your confidence and lead to actual feelings of grief. It's tough to cover up your feelings—but you *have* to in front of the customer. And yet—" He hesitated. "Well, if you don't *express* your grief—somewhere, somehow—it can literally make you sick. Yet, emotionally fit salespeople are capable of experiencing setbacks and disappointments without coming apart."

"What should I do?" asked Jill helplessly. All too recently, she had let her anger boil over, allowing a customer to witness her frustration. She now felt as if she had single-handedly lost the account forever. Was there any way she could recover?

"When dealing with unrealized expectations, rejection, and disappointment, we cycle through a series of emotional states." The Mentor thought a moment, then drew out a sheet of paper. "You must climb the Recovery Ladder."

As Jill and Tim watched, the Mentor drew a pyramid-shaped figure, divided it into five sections between the base and the peak, and drew two arrows pointing up the side of the pyramid.

Then he wrote the words "Shock," "Denial," and "Blame" in the bottom three levels of the pyramid. So it looked like this:

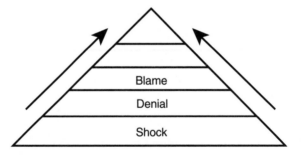

"You see, it's like recovering from a loss. We must first be able to work through the energy-draining feelings of shock, denial, and blame." He looked up. "These feelings are predictable. They're normal—even necessary. And if they are left unexpressed, these feelings will manifest themselves in other settings, whether related or unrelated. It's only through awareness, combined with a conscious act of will, that we can activate the recovery process. That's when you reach the top of the ladder and achieve—"

He paused, then finished off the diagram, adding the words "Acceptance" and "Renewal."

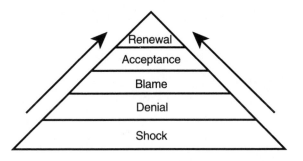

"Shock!" said Jill. "That's exactly what I feel when the customer rejects me."

"It's a violent blow to the mind and emotions," the Mentor concurred. "You're stunned by the rejection. It's just an overwhelming event that comes as a setback. Just consider the impact of that shock—confusion, fear, anger, the feeling that you've been completely knocked off balance. And you probably react with defensiveness and hostility. The reaction is natural—considering how disappointed you feel."

The Mentor pointed to the next stage, denial.

"This is where you're saying to yourself, '*I don't believe I didn't get the business!*' It's a refusal to accept reality—a deliberate refusal to acknowledge what's really happened.

"And what's the impact of denial?" He looked from Tim to Jill.

"Well," said Tim ruefully, "I begin to fantasize that I *did* get the order. I go through a lot of wishful thinking."

The Mentor nodded. "Not surprising, is it? So you probably react with disbelief. You escape into fantasy—painting a scenario different from the one you're actually in."

"And I start blaming others!" Jill put in.

"Yes—that's the next step on the ladder. Blame!" The Mentor pointed to the diagram. Have you ever said, 'You know, I would have been successful *if only I had gotten the support I needed!*'?"

"Even though I know it's not true . . ." Jill agreed.

"It's the 'if-only, if-only' syndrome," said the Mentor. "That's when you find yourself criticizing and condemning your company, your manager, and anybody else who fits into the picture. It's not hard to find the source at this stage of rejection. You're likely to express feelings of hostility, judgmentalism, and defensiveness when you're working through blame."

"And afterward?" inquired Tim.

"Afterward?" The Mentor turned to the diagram again. "Here's acceptance. That's recognizing what *is* and accepting it in place of *what might have been*. And once you've reached that stage, you begin to ask yourself, 'What can I learn from this experience?' and 'How can I learn from losing?' "

"That's when the fog begins to clear—you begin to think clearly again," said Jill.

"It's just dealing with reality—instead of trying to fight it," agreed Tim.

"That's right." The Mentor nodded. "You begin to see a

clearer picture of what happened and what now needs to be done. The moment you reach acceptance, you'll find your stress is reduced as you begin to deal with the pragmatic alternatives. And then you say to yourself, *'Here's what I'm going to do to succeed the next time.'* "

The Mentor pointed to the top of the pyramid, capped by the word "Renewal."

"You set out again, turning your attention to a forward-focused action plan and a renewed sense of purpose."

"That's where *hope* kicks in again," said Tim.

"Exactly," agreed the Mentor. He pushed the paper toward them. "No matter how many times you go through this process, rejection is emotionally wrenching. But you will always recover.

"Experience will help," the Mentor went on. "There are times when you will encounter 'No' with discouraging regularity. The upside of this is that at least you're out there where the action is—making new business development sales calls on target prospects. You'll get used to getting brushed off and turned down. But with experience, you'll find a way to make this a less frequent occurrence. Even though you may feel scolded, you won't run away with your tail tucked between your legs."

"Sometimes the customer's decision almost seems arbitrary," Tim observed.

"Well, some relationships are like a Sadie Hawkins Day dance," the Mentor responded. "It's ladies' choice. You either get picked or you don't get picked."

"But it *really* hurts when you have a lot invested in the relationship," said Tim.

"You mean, you can't stand *losing*," said the Mentor.

"You're right!" Tim laughed. "I can't *stand* it."

"Then you've got my vote of confidence! When you've heard harsh words, suffered crushed hopes, and lost something you fought to gain, it's emotionally expensive. But don't let your despair and disappointment obscure your ability to see clearly and act appropriately."

"Is there a way to speed up recovery?" Jill asked.

"I believe there is." The Mentor nodded.

And then he described The Way.

# ✦✦✦ THE WAY ✦✦✦

✔ **Quiet yourself.**

After a debilitating occurrence, you must accept that you'll feel exhausted, strung out, shocked, and confused. Negative feelings are normal, natural, and necessary. Just don't indulge in them for too long a period of time, or they will pull you down.

Remember, you may be *down* but you're not *out*. In selling, there is no death penalty. You always have the opportunity to rebound—to get up and get on with it. It's not easy to put on a happy face, especially when you're constantly being snubbed, but you can't let rejection influence you to move too cautiously on future sales calls. Once you are rested and have blown off some steam, locate where you are on the Recovery Ladder. Work through that emotional state you find yourself in, and move to acceptance and renewal as quickly as you can.

✔ **Let past victories go to your head.**

You may have to mount a fierce offensive in order to reclaim your lost ground, but you will prevail. Wind the clock back to some of your recent victories. Let the momentum of the last good sales call propel you into the next one and turn the lesson to your advantage. Don't let rejection sap your confidence.

Replace negative self-messages with positive ones: "I didn't get the business this time, but *I will prevail* the next time out." "This is what I'm going to do the next time in order to be successful!"

✔ **Claim your personal power.**

In selling, all too often we resort to coping rather than influencing the outcome of events. Coping is a victim mentality: It's putting up with what is and resigning yourself to bear with it. Influencing, on the other hand, is a leadership behavior. Influencing puts the power back in your hands by converting negative energy caused by losing into the positive energy you need to reposition yourself for winning.

✔ **Level with the customer.**

Clear the air. This will help you take "the high road" and modify the duration, intensity, and impact of the disappointment of not winning the business.

Ask for the opportunity to meet with the customer. Be upbeat, positive, and hopeful.

✔ **Clarify your understanding of the loss.**

This is the action step that tells the customer you care, that you are committed, and that you want to clarify your understanding of the customer's reasons for not choosing you over your rival:

> "Mary, I care a great deal about the relationship that my organization and I have with you as a customer.
>
> "I am committed to doing the very best I can to help you accomplish your goals.
>
> "I am concerned that we were not chosen as your resource.
>
> "Could you clarify my understanding, Mary, by telling me what it was that caused you to choose another alternative?"

Once the customer begins speaking, it is time to listen. This lets the customer know that you are interested and you are determined to continue your efforts.

While you are listening, it is critical that you not only pay heed to what the customer is saying but also to the emotional content of your customer's response. Another way to put this is to get inside the customer's heart as well as his head. This will provide you with insight into why you were not chosen.

Always acknowledge the customer's reasons for not choosing you. This relieves tension and can be done with a nod of the head or a simple, "Yes, I understand."

Make sure you get to the real reasons you were not chosen. Do this by repeating in your own words your understanding of why you were passed over. And ask if your comprehension is realistic and on target.

Once you have the facts straight, renew the relationship: Become partners in creating the next steps that will put you in line for future business. Renewal should result in a series of concrete, forward-focused activities you can take to qualify for future consideration.

Another positive outcome of renewal could be that you are reconsidered for the business you were told you lost. You and the customer can agree upon some steps that you can take to stay in contention for future business or to reposition you for the business you just lost.

It has been my experience that renewing the relationship takes you from waiting and wondering to watching and working.

Being up-front and leveling with the customer is a proactive strategy you can use to reposition yourself for future consideration. It is the best way possible to recover from losing and from finding yourself in an uncertain or negative position. Leveling elevates you to the acceptance and renewal stages in the process of climbing the Recovery Ladder.

Leveling demonstrates poise and class, by permitting you to express your care and concern. It will open up the next steps and create future opportunities.

✦ ✦ ✦

"I'm so relieved," Jill said with a sigh when the Mentor had finished.

"Why?" asked Tim.

"All this time, I thought I was unique in my struggle with feelings of rejection."

"Not at all," replied the Mentor. "Selling is a profession of victories and defeats—of incredible highs and devastating lows. It is a profession that is supercharged with the excitement of accomplishing your sales goals—and the crushing disappointment of losing something you worked hard to obtain."

"Sometimes I come so close—and still lose the sale," Jill responded. "Customers have told me that I make an excellent presentation. But that's a hollow consolation that wears off quickly when I get the sinking feeling that I've lost the deal."

"The same has happened to me," Tim put in.

"For these reasons, it takes a great deal of emotional stamina and courage to sustain yourself during tough times," said the Mentor. "And it takes the will to persevere when you are at your rock-bottom lowest. Dealing effectively with defeat, disappointment, and lost position in selling is one of the single most critical abilities you must acquire.

"If you are not experiencing rejection, then you are on a vacation from selling. As long as you are out there trying to influence change, rejection will be served up on a regular basis.

"But don't ever forget the power of leveling. Often, this effort will help you find a way back to the customer's favor. Leveling takes courage, risky honesty, and skill. It helps you climb the Recovery Ladder."

"I've been selling every day since I got this job," Jill announced, "and I never really learned how to reposition myself as a contender for the business I have lost to my rival. I only wish I had a way to go back to some of my failed attempts and reverse the outcomes."

"You do," replied the Mentor in a soft tone. "There is always the possibility for renewal."

# CHAPTER 15

# RENEW
# YOUR SOUL

# The Key to Renewal

*The forgiving human spirit is often brought to
life in an angry customer—if you're quick
to make amends.*

"I believe you must always be a 'contender for the impossible'," said the Mentor. "Whether you're recovering from the rejection of your solution or you've made a mistake that puts you at risk with the customer, always stay in the game. Remember, customers' needs change so rapidly—and your competitors are so vulnerable—that your chance may come again sooner than you think."

"You know," said Jill, "sometimes I feel like a human punching bag. I never know when I'm going to end up in a toe-to-toe struggle with the customer. Don't they know salespeople are only human?"

The Mentor laughed. "Did anyone ever tell you there's a technical term for mistakes?"

"No. Somehow, I missed that in my education."

"Well, it so happens there is."

"And that term?" Jill inquired.

"The term is screw-ups."

"Screw-ups!" Tim laughed. "That's what they're called, all right."

"Remember, you can have a skirmish in any relationship, no matter how conscientious you try to be," the Mentor went on. "One day, you walk in and there's a total absence of amenities—no 'Hello, how are you? How are things?' Just rudeness and distance. The customer takes an aggressive stance, and the next thing you know you're in a donnybrook. Sometimes, just one incendiary remark or some finger-pointing can set things off."

"And there are customers who blow things all out of proportion," Tim noted. "I feel like some sales calls are booby-trapped—with land mines ready to be detonated."

"Calling on that kind of customer is like making a confession," said the Mentor. "You really don't want to listen to bitter recriminations, but you're afraid what might happen if you don't."

"You certainly put your finger on it," said Jill. "I call it sniper alley. Some customers seem like such hard people to please, and some treat you with an iron hand. They break your heart day in and day out. They're abrasive and arrogant. I've been at the receiving end of some blistering scoldings. It seems so hopelessly unfair. It's not even *mis*treatment. It's *mal*treatment."

"Sometimes, you know the treatment is just patently unjust," the Mentor observed. "I've received bitter, intense scoldings I never deserved. On the other hand, I have to admit that most of my problems were self-imposed. I anticipated the worst—and that's exactly what I got. Wearing a brave smile, I would adopt a siege mentality and prepare to joust with the customer. I became defensive before I ever really found out what the problem was.

"I remember one customer. . . ." The Mentor shook his head.

"A happy memory?" Tim laughed.

"He went at me with dagger drawn. He was combative and vindictive. He passed the point where his insults and taunts were sporadic—they turned into routine behavior, and I had to bear the brunt of it. My sales calls on this person were so dangerous, I had to wear a protective shield. And I was ill-prepared to handle his hostile remarks and stubborn objections. Any time I approached him, I felt like I was in for a lynching. When the tough talk began, it was clear his anger was aimed at me. And I felt as if I was constantly scrambling to get out of his way so I wouldn't get slapped around. His rebukes were extreme to the point of being excessive. No matter how I braced myself for getting roughed up, I was always seared by his criticism."

"How could you stand it?" Tim was horrified. "Didn't you just want to—fight back?"

"Indeed, I did. Sometimes, seeing this customer was like being gripped in a trance of anger. I had to remain composed, alert, and not distracted when he dug in his heels. It was one of my single most difficult challenges. I was depressed. I was seething. And I'm sorry to say I resorted to a garden variety of dysfunctional behaviors."

"You—mad?" Jill regarded the Mentor with disbelief.

The Mentor frowned deeply at the memory. "I'd go into a state of high alert—then angrily deny the customer's complaints or accusations. And then . . . I would lose it! I would get angry. We had some real face-offs."

He looked from Tim to Jill. The regret in his voice demanded unequivocal respect.

"My miscalculated and erroneous estimate of the situation would send me into a mindless rage, setting off a raft of negative reactions."

"And—what if you said nothing? Just let the customer vent?" Tim wondered.

"If only," the Mentor sighed. "Unfortunately for me, keeping my mouth shut was rarely an option. If I didn't respond—*react* is the better word—I felt like a person with both hands tied behind my back. I reacted like a condemned man. I let the customer pass sentence and then protested fiercely. I had to learn—well, above all, I had to learn how to stay in control and not let the other person's hostile reaction to *me* hook me into similar behavior toward *him*."

The Mentor paused for a moment to reflect. "Of course, not *all* difficult customers are difficult in the same way."

"You bet they're not!" Tim exclaimed. "But we all know the sales calls we dread the most. There's the 'touch-off' guy who goes off like a bomb if anybody lights his fuse. The 'warden'—hands folded tightly, wearing a grim face, he's got the stoic composure of a prison guard. Or the 'executioner'— if you don't toe the line, you'll face the music."

"But even your best and kindest customers can make you feel as if you've made a career-shattering mistake if you screw up," Jill said.

"A serious mistake can hound you," the Mentor agreed. "And it can have far-reaching consequences. In fact, it can wreak enormous havoc if it happens with distressing frequency. If you accept the calamity with apathy, you may find the customer's low-grade anger escalates into full-blown, angry exchanges punctuated by harsh words.

"If the problem goes unresolved or you blow it off, deep dissatisfaction will set in," the Mentor went on. "Don't let the situation become desperate. If there is widespread agreement that you are not doing the job, you might just as well be on a sinking ship. Don't be surprised if a customer who is sore at you seeks indemnity. He wants you to pay for the screw-ups."

"The worst is when you have to make excuses," Jill said.

"So, whatever happened to that customer you described—the one who gave you such a hard time?" Tim wondered aloud.

"Oh, him!" The Mentor smiled. "We patched it up. He's one of my best customers—and my favorite person to call on."

"What brought about *that* turnaround?"

"Well, it was no instant miracle. In fact, it took years." The Mentor regarded them steadily. "Listen, you two—you might as well hear it now. You never want to be on bad terms with a customer—ever. But asking for forgiveness, asking to be given another chance, can be a pain-filled process.

"You know, most salespeople are not done in by their competitors, but rather by themselves. They give up on a tough customer too soon.

"I'd like to think that the customers you call on are naturally good, supportive, and anxious to hear you out and help you fix the screw-up. Regrettably, in many cases the reverse is true. Customers will be closed down, impatient, harsh, angry, and unkind."

"You'd think customers would learn something, too," Jill mused. "Like, how to get the most value from the sales professionals they're dealing with."

"We can wish," the Mentor agreed. "The reality is, in the

future the customer will have to do more with less—that is, with less money and time. They will view screw-ups with a more trained and critical eye. They will be quick to quantify the financial cost of your mistake and hold you accountable. Customers may take a hard-line stance against giving you another chance if they have been let down too many times. Their hearts will harden, and they'll stiffen their resolve to correct a recurring problem. In fact, if you really screw up, you may meet your permanent replacement passing you as you're on your way out the door."

"I wish I had some technique—some *way* to address customers' problems so the situation doesn't turn into a sparring match," remarked Tim. "So often, it feels like a contest of wills."

The Mentor flashed a smile of satisfaction that told Tim and Jill—as plainly as words—that he was prepared to answer that request.

"I happen to carry a model in my heart and in my head," said the Mentor. "It has served me well."

"What's it look like?" asked Jill.

"Well, it's really just four circles. And in each circle is a single letter."

And the Mentor drew it for them:

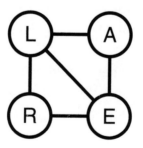

"And the words that go with it?" Tim felt a sense of anticipation, as if he was on the threshold of some new domain.

"You've heard the words already," said the Mentor, "but this will help you remember." He pointed to the circle that was marked with an "L." "That's for Listen," he observed. Pointing to the other circles in sequence, the Mentor continued, "Then there's Acknowledge. Explore. And Respond."

"Listen?" Tim wondered aloud.

"To be a good listener, you have to have an unfailing ear and a generous spirit. Listening is the life-support system when you're resolving conflict, because the act of listening says to the customer, 'I regret what happened; I want the details; I want to fix the problem.' "

"But how can you get that across—if you're just *listening*?" Jill wondered.

"The key is what you're doing *while* you're listening," the Mentor replied. "You can acknowledge the customer's problem with a concerned facial expression, or a thoughtful gesture. Couple this with a supportive reply, like, 'I understand—you have a valid point.' Or, 'I regret this problem happened.' Acknowledging also includes showing appreciation to the customer for bringing the problem to your attention.

"If you do this, you have adopted a tone that suggests you are genuinely interested, that you care, and that you want to be helpful in solving the problem."

"But the problem's still not solved!" Tim frowned. "The customer always wants to know, 'What are you going to do about this? How are you going to *fix* it?' "

"And that's when many salespeople are tempted to grandstand."

"Grandstand?" Jill looked puzzled.

"You know: You say, 'I'll take care of this.' You grab the phone, call someone in the office, blast them out, and turn to the customer and say, 'There, all fixed.' " The Mentor paused. "The only trouble with that is, you're sending a very different message. You're letting the customer know you're impatient with his problem; you don't want to handle it yourself; you want to blame someone else. By grandstanding, by focusing on the fix-it side, you are leaving out the important step of exploring the customer's problem."

"Well, then, what's the next step?" asked Tim.

"The next step is to explore for further information and then verify that your understanding of the problem is complete and accurate. It could go something like this: 'In other words, the problem we are dealing with is as follows'—and you state it in your own words, exactly as you understand it. And then ask, 'Is my understanding complete and accurate?'

"If you get an affirmative from the customer and you're certain you understand the problem, you're in a position to respond, 'Now that I understand the problem, I recommend the following corrective action steps to fix the current situation and to prevent the problem in the future.' "

"That seems so diplomatic," Jill ventured.

The Mentor laughed. "Maybe that's all diplomacy is. Listening to understand. Acknowledging the difficulty the customer is having. Exploring the reason behind the mishap. Then responding with a constructive action. There you have it." He shrugged. "Those four steps provide the key to addressing customers' problems in a helpful way. Listen, Acknowledge, Explore, and Respond."

"Then that's all?"

"Well—there's a bit more to it than that," the Mentor responded. "When you've got a problem with the customer, you need to learn to manage your emotional state of mind. Holding on to anger and bitterness contaminates your ability to view the situation realistically. Bitterness floods your consciousness with negative thoughts that blind you. When you're bitter, you can't stay focused on the problem you're trying to solve. An investment of common sense pays off in significant dividends. If you want to rescue the relationship, you need to take quick and vigorous action."

"What kind of action?" Tim asked.

"Here are the steps," the Mentor said. And he began to outline The Way.

## ♦♦♦ THE WAY ♦♦♦

✔ **Exercise restraint.**

Be the one who calls a cessation of hostilities. You need to avoid choking the relationship with a hostile reaction to the customer's harshness. Anger disrupts your concentration, and that results in impaired performance. You need to rescue yourself beforehand from the predictable consequences of anger. Remember, disasters are reversible.

✔ **Be patient.**

There are times when you have to cope with the bullying tactics of a hostile customer who is upset with your performance. Don't let it lead to a showdown. Show some class, and take the high road—that is, the calm, reasonable approach, even when you are disappointed and seething.

✔ **Adopt a helpful tone.**

Even though there will be times when the customer's behavior is both harsh and critical, there is always something positive you can do. Look for a bridge back to the good graces of your customer. Admit your mistake, fix it for good, and move on. Reassure the customer that you will take a corrective action step.

✔ **Avoid a contentious showdown.**

Be aware of your own confrontational tactics like scowling, folding your arms, or giving the customer an icy glare. Don't become hot-tempered under fire—or an argument could turn into a sparring match of wits. Shift away from a showdown.

✔ **Turn the other cheek.**

Turning the other cheek is not introverted aggression. It's aggression transformed into a strategy for winning in the long run. Reconcile your differences sooner rather than later, before a residue of lingering resentment begins to build.

✔ **Take the cool, reasonable approach.**

When you are disappointed and you come under hostile cross-examination, call a permanent cease-fire. Even if you're full of pent-up anger and ready to blow your stack, put a muzzle on your mouth. By doing this, you are operating at a high level of consciousness.

✔ **Work with what's possible.**

In your attempts to restore good relations, you may encounter stiff resistance. Don't become a victim of your own inaction. Go in with an olive branch held in your hand and hoist it in the air. The customer may be waiting to forgive you and give you another chance, but you will never know unless you call.

✔ **Don't let your stomach take charge.**

If you lose your composure during a sales transaction, you have lost your rudder. You will wander off in a variety of directions with no clear-cut goal in mind. Get back on course by listening, acknowledging, exploring, and responding. Don't put your head on hold while you let your stomach take charge.

✔ **Stay tuned to the customer's tone.**

If you truly listen, you'll find that he'll soften his tone. It won't help you to run for cover—though that's what you may feel like doing if you're in the throes of emotional distress. You can make restitution and take some of your power back—if you work through adversity and make a renewed commitment.

✔ **Stay objective, alert, and helpful.**

That means avoiding hostility and anger—which could diminish your capacity to do that. Ask yourself the question: "Will I deal more effectively with this situation if I'm upset?" When you realize your anger won't help you, objectivity comes more easily.

✔ **Start with a clean slate.**

Look for the telltale signs that you are starting to lose it. When a customer is being unreasonable and making your life miserable for no good reason, you might need a cooling-off period. Take a breath of fresh air. Quiet yourself. Approach the customer when you are rested and refreshed.

✔ **Get the help of your support team.**

Sometimes, it's your organization's support system—not you—that's let the customer down. But if you fight your own system, you might as well cut your legs off. Instead, go back and coach your system into helping you do a better job for the customer.

✔ **Repair the mistake.**

A quick and momentary flurry of activity won't do it. You must employ urgently needed remedial action. Your high-energy efforts will serve as a strong expression of your desire and your will to put things right. Refocus your attention on the issue that is causing the problem and fortify your resolve to fix the situation.

✔ **Move on!**

When you've made a mistake, be willing to accept the consequences of your actions. Make peace with yourself and move on.

✦ ✦ ✦

Jill exchanged a brief glance with Tim. When their eyes met, Tim realized that Jill was as stunned as he was by the Mentor's words. It was as if the Mentor had perceived all the frustration, anger, and embarrassment that was part of their lives. And by acknowledging that he, too, shared such emotions, he made them seem less frightening.

It was a fitting conclusion to all they had heard from the Mentor—and Tim felt as satisfied as if he had just shared a meal at a bountiful table. He felt grateful—and he could tell by Jill's expression that her feelings were the same.

As for the Mentor: From the expressions on the faces of his listeners, he could tell that the strain of the past weeks and months had taken its toll. He tried to recall what the world of business had been like when he began. Sure, the pressures had been there—and the long hours—and the ambition to succeed.

But now, he could see, something else had entered the picture—a larger factor of uncertainty than ever before. In some ways, Tim and Jill were better equipped than any generation before them to face the challenges of the business world. They were well educated, technically proficient.

Yet in other ways they were hungry and needy. They needed the patience and guidance of an older, wiser guide who had weathered the ups and downs of many cycles. They sought an anchor in a sea of change—and their lack of firm guidance and belief was taking its toll on their personal lives as well as their professional lives.

What lay ahead of them?

With a sigh, the Mentor rose to his feet.

"Thank you!" The gratitude was palpable in Jill's voice. "But we've taken enough of your time."

"I hope you'll take more," said the Mentor.

"It's funny," observed Tim, "but I feel like some kind of weight has been lifted from my shoulders. I don't know what it is. When we came in here, I thought I was ready to drop. Now—well, I'm just brimming with ideas about things I'd like to do tomorrow."

"That's energy." The Mentor laughed. "It was there all along. Maybe I just mentioned some ways to direct it."

"More than that!" Jill responded. "I feel like I'm really beginning to understand—at last."

The Mentor regarded her with compassion.

"You know," he said, "I think all of us have a capacity for greatness—but having it and using it are two different things. In the final analysis, *you* decide how successful you are going to be—nobody else." He studied them for a moment. "It's absolutely necessary to look inside yourself and ask the question, 'Can I program myself to win?'"

"Some people *do* seem programmed to win," Tim observed.

"I agree," replied the Mentor.

"Can you tell which ones?" asked Jill.

"Well, I can tell you that winners have a positive self-image. They see themselves as worthy and as making a difference in other people's lives. When you're a winning businessperson or sales professional, you view yourself as a valued resource to your customers."

"Anything else you've observed?" asked Tim.

"Yes." The Mentor reflected a moment. "Winners are ambitious, dependable, and inspired workers. They are sound of mind and, without exception, they appreciate the value of sound work-ethic habits. They love their work, demonstrate high energy, and are creatively focused.

"The best of the best don't judge others," the Mentor went on. "Rather, they are accepting. They have good things to say about everything and everyone. They possess a generous heart, and they are capable of loving others into changing. They *are anam cara.*"

The Mentor seemed to lose his train of thought for a moment.

"Come on," he said. "I'm ready to go."

Picking up his briefcase and raincoat, the Mentor followed Tim and Jill through the door. They headed down the long corridor toward the elevator.

"You know," he said while they waited, "I wish every person in this building could identify and actively employ the qualities they appreciate and value most about themselves. If all of us could just replace self-defeating thoughts with a positive self-message."

The elevator doors opened, and the Mentor signaled Tim and Jill to precede him.

"What should the first message be?" the Mentor asked.

"I'm going to be great today!" Tim and Jill said in unison—and they both laughed.

"That's a good start," the Mentor rejoined. That was all he said until some time later when they were standing outside the front door, prepared to part ways.

"Both of you have the qualities you need," he said, turning to them. "Before you know it, you will be influencing standards by which your competitors are judged. You will control and manage the playing field."

"That's hard to believe right now," said Tim.

"I know it is." He turned to leave, then thought of something and turned back to them. "Maybe there's something I forgot to mention." Even in the dim light, Tim could see there was a twinkle in the Mentor's eye. "You're both winners," the Mentor went on. "*Both* of you," he insisted more emphatically. "You love your work. You've got high energy. You're creatively focused. You're ambitious, dependable, and inspired. And not only that, you're both good listeners." He thought to himself a moment before adding, "I just hope we can keep you. I just hope we can."

An instant later, he was gone into the night, nothing but the echo of his reassurance remaining where he had once stood.

But the echo was as clear to Tim and Jill as if the Mentor were still standing before them, speaking aloud.

"We're going to win," said Tim. "He said we're going to win."

"And we are!" exclaimed Jill. "We have The Way."

JACK CAREW is the founder and chief executive officer of Carew International, a global training-and-development organization. Jack is a visionary in the field of sales and management, and the programs offered by Carew International are recognized as the pinnacle of excellence in sales and development.

Carew International, Inc.
659 Van Meter Street
Cincinnati, OH 45202-1568

Phone: (800) 227-3977 or (513) 621-0229
Fax: (513) 621-0876
http://www.carew.com/